So Many Books, So Little Time

A Year of Passionate Reading

B

BERKLEY BOOKS

NEW YORK

THE BERKLEY PUBLISHING GROUP
Published by the Penguin Group
Penguin Group (USA) Inc
375 Hudson Street, New York, New York 10014, USA
Penguin Group (Canada), 10 Alcorn Avenue, Toronto, Ontario M4V 3B2, Canada
(a division of Pearson Penguin Canada Inc.)
Penguin Group Ltd., 80 Strand, London WC2R 0RL, England
Penguin Group Ireland, 25 St. Stephen's Green, Dublin 2, Ireland (a division of Penguin Books Ltd.)
Penguin Group (Australia), 250 Camberwell Road, Camberwell, Victoria 3124, Australia
(a division of Pearson Australia Group Pty. Ltd.)
Penguin Books India Pvt. Ltd., 11 Community Centre, Panchsheel Park, New Delhi—110 017, India
Penguin Group (NZ), Cnr. Airborne and Rosedale Roads, Albany, Auckland 1310, New Zealand
(a division of Pearson New Zealand Ltd.)
Penguin Books (South Africa) (Pty.) Ltd., 24 Sturdee Avenue, Rosebank, Johannesburg 2196,
South Africa

Penguin Books Ltd., Registered Offices: 80 Strand, London WC2R 0RL, England

PRINTING HISTORY
G. P. Putnam's Sons hardcover edition / October 2003
Berkley trade paperback edition / October 2004

Berkley trade paperback ISBN: 0-425-19819-7

The Library of Congress has cataloged the
G. P. Putnam's Sons hardcover edition as follows:

Nelson, Sara, date.
So many books, so little time :
a year of passionate reading / Sara Nelson.
p.   cm.
ISBN 0-399-15083-8
1. Books and reading—United States.
2. Nelson, Sara—Books and reading.   I. Title.
Z1003.2.N45   2003   2003043222
028'.9'0973—dc21

PRINTED IN THE UNITED STATES OF AMERICA
10 9 8 7 6 5 4 3 2 1

Most Berkley Books are available at special quantity discounts for bulk purchases for sales
promotions, premiums, fund-raising, or educational use. Special books, or book excerpts, can
also be created to fit specific needs.

For details, write: Special Markets, The Berkley Publishing Group, 375 Hudson Street,
New York, New York 10014.

"Written for book junkies like me. It is a feast and a road map to great literature and its polar opposite. Sara Nelson reads well, thinks sharply, and delivers the goods." —Pat Conroy

"This book is bliss . . . Whatever your subject, you have to treat it with 'fearlessness, attitude and energy,' writes Nelson, and she goes at books with this same unbeatable combination." —*The Boston Globe*

"Any reader's ticket to bliss. What a joy this chronicle is! Sara Nelson is a splendid writer—smart, witty, tough-minded, and kindhearted. Book lovers everywhere are sure to add *So Many Books, So Little Time* to their list of favorites." —Susan Isaacs

"Part memoir, part bibliophile's exploration of great novels, overhyped classics, and the occasional brilliant piece of good luck. Nelson lovingly blends her life and literature, and makes me want to crawl through the dust jacket and curl up with a list of my own." —Linda Fairstein

"A smart and delightful celebration of one of civilized life's essential pleasures. What sort of person picks up a book in a bookstore and checks out the little promotional blurbs . . . ? A person like you, obviously—someone who enjoys looking at books, enjoys thinking about books, enjoys reading. If you also happen to respond well to laugh-out-loud wit, passionate opinions, deeply charming candor and unpretentious wisdom, then Sara Nelson is your perfect companion." —Kurt Andersen

"For those who devour books, a porterhouse, perfectly rare. Or, if you prefer, an enormous bowl of paper-thin handmade potato chips. A smart, witty, utterly original memoir about how every book becomes a part of us." —Augusten Burroughs, author of *Running with Scissors* and *Dry*

"A marvelous record of how books choose us more than we choose them and how they then proceed to have a wonderful impact on our lives . . . a work that will make readers run to the shelf to discover which book beckons next. Recommended." —*Library Journal*

"Nelson is highlighting a central aspect of reading often ignored by critics. We all look for ourselves in books. And just as we always see faces in clouds, we can find ourselves in almost any work." —Scripps Howard News Service

Sara Nelson

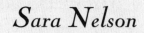

To Charles Nelson,
1917 - 1990, who didn't know
what he was getting himself into when
he taught me to read all those years ago
and
To Charley Yoshimura,
who lives with the result, every day

Acknowledgments

Like Groucho Marx, who knew he couldn't do any horsewhipping if he didn't have a horse, I am first and most grateful to all the authors and publishers out there who've produced the books without which this book could never have been written. Even when I don't like something I've read, I'm glad that I read it—most of the time, anyway—and I owe you all for that.

On the other hand, Groucho also said, more famously, that he wouldn't belong to any club that would have him as a member. With this, I profoundly disagree; I consider myself very lucky to have lived and worked with a lot of different people, in a lot of different clubs, and to have been accepted by a lot of them a lot of the time. There are many I can't thank by name, because I don't know their names, but I've recorded their offhand, funny, and often inspiring comments about books and a whole lot of other stuff.

But here is a partial list of the ones I do know, the ones who are welcome at my club, anytime: my agent, Mark Reiter, who saw the possibilities in a book about reading almost before I did, and my editor, Neil Nyren, who generously jumped at the chance to publish it; and my friends and colleagues Nan Jones, Jake Morrissey, Alexia Brue, Annik LaFarge, Adrian Zackheim, David Hirshey, Gil Schwartz, Jessie Woeltz, Judy Coyne, Judy Stone, Kathy Rich, Mary Duenwald, Elisabeth Egan, Lindsey Turner, Leigh Haber, Trena Keating, Marjorie Braman, John Martini, Laura Mathews, Andy Russem, Bill Goldstein, Lynn Goldberg, Louisa Ermelino, Stephen "Kuff" Nelson, Jonathan Nelson, Joanne Kaufman, Sarah Crichton, Rachel Clarke, Lorraine Shanley, Constance Sayre, Robert Sabbag, Ira Silverberg, Hazel Shillingford, Lizz Winstead, Ruth Liebmann, Robin Wolaner, Lindy Hess, Miwa Messer, Jake Brown, Ellen Ryder, Maura Fritz, Dennis Wurst, Leah Rosch, John Kaye; everybody from Inside.com, particularly David Carr, Stephen Battaglio, PJ Mark, and Kurt Andersen; everybody at *Glamour*, particularly Cindi Leive, Alison Brower, Kristin Van Ogtrop, Jill Herzig, Erin Zammett, and Allison Mezzafonte; everybody at *The New York Observer*, particularly Maria Russo and Peter Kaplan; and of course, the St. Luke's Moms, particularly Maria Turgeon, Lauren Turner, Kara Young, Sabrina Turin, Paulette Bogan, Jane Stewart, and Susan Holmes.

I especially want to thank the following, without whose daily support, advice, and faith I'd still be on page 1:

James Ireland Baker, not only a find of a friend but a reader and writer extraordinaire.

Liza Nelson, for a sisterhood that rarely exists outside of books.

June Nelson, for an amazing example.

And Leo Akira Yoshimura, the only person I know who can describe me as "relentless" and mean it as a compliment.

Contents

So Many Books,
So Little Time

Prologue

C all me Insomniac.

It's three A.M. and as usual, I'm awake, wandering around my New York apartment. I stumble toward the space my husband and son call the family room but I privately think of as "my library." From floor to ceiling on three walls, it's beautifully lined with cherry shelves. My husband, Leo—a production designer for *Saturday Night Live*, and somebody who knows a thing or three hundred about woodworking—built these for me with husbandly pride, professional exactitude, and only a modicum of marital resignation. "Just don't ask me to do the same for your shoes," he said.

I love this room and have spent hundreds of late-night hours here surrounded by my books. There's the set of proofs I kept putting off for two years until I met—and adored—its author at a party. There's the novel by a writer I knew of only by reputation, until he became my favorite boss. Then there's the out-of-print biography I scoured the Web to find—and finally scored from a used-book dealer in Denver.

I've spent more than late-night time in this room. I've also expended lots of thought and energy here, reading novels I'd saved up for just the right moment, fretting that my books would soon outgrow the precious personal real estate Leo had provided for them, worrying that some favorite book had gone missing, even briefly attempting mass alphabetization. You might not be able to figure out what's going on here organizationally, but I have a Rain Man–like capacity to visualize the books, almost title by title, and put my hand on any one within seconds. If I have an urge to dip into, say, John Hubner's *Bottom Feeders*, an odd biography of the San Francisco pornographers the Mitchell brothers, I see it in my mind's eye, nestled next to Sheri Holman's *The Dress Lodger* at the bottom of the shelf behind me. There's no discernible logic for those two very different books' existing as neighbors except, perhaps, that they both have bluish covers.

But tonight, unlike most nights, I have an agenda. Tomorrow I'm leaving for a visit to my friend Sabrina's house in Vermont, and I need to choose a book to take with me. I have a New Year's plan: I'm setting out to read a book a week for the next year and write a diary of the experience.

"A book a week?" some friends have asked, shaking their heads in what I blithely assume is envy. "How are you going to do that while you also have a job, a son, and a life to live?" But until now, I haven't been worried. For twenty years, as I worked as a reporter, a teacher, an editor, a TV producer, a book reviewer, and a freelance magazine writer—and for seven as a mother—I've been reading, and usually way more than a book a week. I'm ravenous for books and awake half of most nights—a good combination, it turns out, since the best reading time is from three to five A.M. in this very room.

You should know that I wasn't always like this. I mean, I've always been a night crawler, but there were periods of my life when the rooms I crawled through were a little more populated—and a whole lot louder—than my lovely library is today. I used to go to movies almost compulsively. One of my favorite things, as a teenager, was to spend weekend afternoons at what we quaintly, in those small-town pre-multiplex days, called double features. I used to go on dates, until I met Leo fourteen years ago and our marriage put an end to *that*, at least more or less. I used to go, honest to God, dancing. I wasn't, in short, the kind of egghead graduate student who showed up at the publishing programs I've taught at over the years, kids who claimed their love of reading dated back to toddlerhood, when a book fell from the shelves onto their tiny heads and they wiped off the blood and opened the book and *voilà*, their lives were changed forever.

I wasn't a particularly early reader or even a very avid one; I don't have bittersweet memories of sitting by the window devouring *Little House on the Prairie* as other kids whooped it up in the playground. I never once, as an adolescent, chose a fictional Heathcliff over my personal real-life version, who was a boy named Brett Friedman who looked more like Mick Jagger. I was a good student, sure, but I was motivated more by a need to please the teachers (and my parents) than by any love of literature. In other words, when it came to reading, I did what I was told: *Moby-*

Dick required in the eighth grade? No problem. Luckily, I was always a fast reader, which meant I still usually had time to busy myself with my more "interactive" pursuits, like torturing my little brother and perfecting my role as the family crybaby.

And when I did read for personal pleasure instead of academic profit, I wanted escape, not enlightenment. I remember, for example, a period immediately post-college when my best friend (who was soon to become my biggest rival) landed one of her first freelance magazine assignments. She was to read and review a novel, *Enchantment*, by the longtime *New Yorker* writer Daphne Merkin. Apparently, this was a serious novel that made some important points about growing up in America, but I would never have known it had another friend not chosen to rub my face in it: "She's reading that, and what are you reading?" she chided. "Jackie Collins?"

I'll still never understand how she knew.

In other words, through most of my life, up to and including now, there are holes in my reading experience wide enough to drive the proverbial Mack truck through. I read a lot in college, of course, but my major was Latin American Studies (I had an affinity for foreign languages) instead of the more usual English. Consequently, I'd read a lot of the magical realists and just about no Dickens. My specialty, in fact, was obscure Latin American poets, like the Chilean Cubist Vicente Huidobro, but I knew nothing of, say, Keats. In fact, all I could have told you about that poet's famous odes was a joke my older brother Kuff used to make at the dinner table. What's a Grecian urn? He'd ask. Answer: About a buck an hour.

So when did my life change? Looking back, I can see the early warning signs of readaholism, like when my mother gave me *Marjorie Morningstar* when I was thirteen and I pulled an all-nighter reading—and weeping over—the Herman Wouk novel. I remember one long and lonely summer just before college when I worked as a Kelly Girl in Boston and turned up at my only local friend's house every weekend with a different novel. ("You're reading *The Golden Notebook?*" I remember her saying. "Last week it was Paul Bowles!") But I guess I'd say my "disease" reached full flower soon after I'd started living alone in New York, with little money and a narrow social circle that included not-so-friendly friends like the ones above. Slowly, it dawned on me: Books could be more than a path to good grades or something to do when, in those pre-cable days, you'd already seen the Movie of the Week.

I started paying closer attention to book reviews and began taking advantage of the free review copies that were pouring into the magazine at which I worked as an editorial assistant. I didn't have much to do on weekends anyway, so I began cruising bookstores and got myself a New York Public Library card. And soon I was hooked: not only were books cheaper than movies and easier to find than suitable human dates, they could take me with them to fabulous places. I could be sitting in my dank studio apartment with five dollars to my name, but simply by opening a book, I could be in Paris in the nineteenth century. I started to beg, borrow, or buy just about any novel, biography, or memoir I could find. I even went through a period when I turned my knowledge of obscure Latin American literature into a tiny—and I mean minuscule—cottage industry by translating a couple of novels and poems for which I was handsomely rewarded with sums, as Calvin Trillin once said, in the high two figures.

Don't get me wrong: I eventually did start to have a life, plenty of work and friends and trips and movies and dramas—of the interpersonal, not just the bookish, kind. Nobody who knows me would ever confuse me with Marian the Librarian ("Why, Miss Nelson, when you take off your glasses, you're actually pretty!") or suggest I left a single social stone unturned in my pursuit of literature. In fact, I think it's just the opposite: the busier I've gotten over the years—the more family and work activities, the more friends to keep up with, the more duties of adulthood and parenthood, the more, well, *life*—the more, not the less, I've read. Maybe I'm perverse, but there's something comforting to me about knowing that whatever is going on in my outer world, bad or good, exciting or boring, I know I will find comfort and joy and excitement the minute I get home to my book *du jour* or *semaine* or, very rarely, *mois*.

So reading a book a week doesn't scare me, exactly, though I do get kind of anxious when somebody asks the next question: "But how will you pick your books?" While I glibly, proudly, always respond, "The same way everybody else does," the truth is, I'm not sure. Will I ask friends for recommendations? (As it turns out, yes. A lot.) Will I cruise bookstores? (Uh-huh.) Will I read reviews? (Less so. I was once a reviewer, so I know better.) I've already made a list of all the things I always meant to get to and never did, and a few titles I loved that I want to reread.[1] It's a pretty long list, and

---

[1] See Appendix A.

if I worry aloud about anything, it's that there will be too many books to fill the year.

But here's the question nobody asks me, the one I've been asking myself, privately, in the silence of my bed and head. What, exactly, am I doing this *for*? Why, exactly, do I read so much and what, exactly, do I expect to get out of chronicling my reading? I'm not planning to write fifty-two book reviews. I'm not trying to meet or set some standard of what it means to be well read. I couldn't care less about telling you what to read. What I am doing, I think, is trying to get down on paper what I've been doing for years in my mind: matching up the reading experience with the personal one and watching where they intersect—or don't. If a particular book I mention makes you want to head off to the nearest bookstore, great; if not, maybe what I say about it will spark a memory or suggest a topic that seems honest or interesting or true.

Years ago I interviewed the singer (and now author) Rosanne Cash about her career. We started talking about specific songs she'd written and performed, and I found myself saying to her that a certain ballad reminded me of my boyfriend from college or that another one took me right back to a guy I was dating at another time. After I'd made a couple such references, I apologized for all this personalizing; surely there was more to say about her music than how it interacted with my love life. But Cash—whom, I confess, I can only dream of being a little bit like—laughed. "That's what I do, too," she said. "That's what you're supposed to do. If a song gets to you personally, then it's a really good song."

Well, books get to me personally. They remind me of the person I was and the people I knew at the time I read them, the places

Sara Nelson

I visited, the dreams I had as I lay on the couch or in bed or on the beach and read them. I can stand in front of my cherry shelves and point to an obscure title—let's say that biography, *Bottom Feeders*—and tell you where I got it (from an Internet bookstore), why (because I saw a not completely favorable but definitely provocative review in the paper), and what I thought when I started reading it (that it reminded me of the semester I spent on leave from college living in what my mother insists was a San Francisco commune but was really just a house with roommates). I talk about my books as if they were people, and I choose them the way I choose my friends: because somebody nice introduced us, because I liked their looks, because the best of them turn out to be smart and funny and both surprising and inevitable at the same time.

Charley has just begun second grade, and Leo his twenty-seventh season of the show; I've just started a new part-time job at a magazine. My mother, God willing, will turn eighty-five before my year is done. Obviously, I don't know what's going to happen in the coming months, either on the global or personal level. But the one thing I do know is that no matter what does happen, I'll be reading through it, as I always have. And if I know me, I'll be connecting the dots as usual: trying to figure out why I read what I read when I read it, how one book leads to another, and, of course, what it all means about me, my life, and the nature of reading itself.

"I've given up reading books," the American humorist Oscar Levant once wrote. "I find it takes my mind off myself."

Poor Oscar. He missed the point.

January 6
Great Expectations

B
ut enough about me. Let's talk about my project.

I'm here trying to choose my first book of the year. I've spent a good couple of days thinking about what that book should be, which means I've been scanning these shelves as well as sifting through the piles near my bed, the ones mentally marked Must Read, Might Read, and Maybe Someday. (I'm intermittently ruthless about the assignment of these categories, banishing Richard Russo's *Empire Falls* from Must Read to Maybe Someday after six failed attempts to get interested in it. On the other hand, I moved Laura Hillenbrand's *Seabiscuit* from Might Read to Must Read after no fewer than six friends extolled its virtues.) I've already decided to take one biggish book instead of the usual three or four I often pack as insurance against being caught—can you imagine?—with nothing to read. I've already finished *The Corrections*—and besides, I have this idea that the New Year should begin with a New Book, preferably one that's light and maybe even funny. The year 2001 was tough going for all of us, and I have this superstitious idea that if I start this year with something happy, it'll be a happy year.

Eventually, I find, high up on the shelves, where the newest books often go, a copy of *Funnymen*, a novel by Ted Heller, who wrote the delightful *Slab Rat*, which I loved, despite the terrible review it got in *The New York Times Book Review.* Heller—son of Joseph *Catch-22* Heller—has a gift for black comedy (coincidence or genetics? You decide), and this new novel sounds intriguing: it's an imagined oral history of a comedy team made up of a Jewish comedian and an Italian-American crooner in the post-vaudeville era. It's a Martin–Lewis kind of thing, I gather from the jacket copy, and while I've never been a great fan of that particular couple, I find the phenomenon kind of interesting. And it weighs in at around 400 pages, so all my criteria are met. *Funnymen* it is, then, I think as I tuck it into my duffel bag.

I should probably stop right here and explain that this wasn't the most ordinary of Vermont lodges we would be visiting. Our host, my friend Sabrina, is the widow of a stepson of the famous Russian writer and thinker Alexander Solzhenitsyn. As mother of the author's first grandchild, Sabrina is still welcome at the compound in Cavendish, Vermont, where the Solzhenitsyns lived in exile for nearly twenty years. (They're now back in Russia, and the Cavendish digs are used by Sabrina and the two S. sons who live in the States.) The idea of visiting a famous Nobel Prize–winning author's home appeals to me, and besides, Sabrina has promised us skiing lessons and hot toddies and lots and lots of lazy hours to read by the fire.

When we get there, the family's choice of exile venue begins to make sense: it's beautiful land up here, but isolated, and very, very cold. The two houses the author had built for him—one for the family to live in and one for the writer to write in—are connected by a basement passageway. There's something very Russian about the whole setup, and it even suggests a kind of architectural Stockholm syndrome: the expatriate author purposely building a home reminiscent of the Siberian prison in which he spent a couple of decades.

In other words, it's the polar (pun intended) opposite of the warm, loquacious nightclub world Heller portrays in *Funnymen*.

Still, I'm looking forward to the visit and to reading *Funnymen*, and after a day on the slopes—or rather, a day in which Leo and I hovered as Charley took his first skiing lesson on the slopes—a hearty dinner, and a couple of drinks, I sit down on the simple sofa in front of the fire and open it. But suddenly, it's not so Funny. In the book, Heller is describing the honky-tonk vaudevillian atmosphere of a Catskills nightclub; I look up for a moment and see hard ground and bare, frozen trees. One character refers to the "A-bomb" nature of the act because it "kills" so well, and I wander into the Russian Orthodox chapel the author built for himself in the basement. I'm sorting through characters named Heine and Ziggy and Snuffy and my eyes wander to the wall-to-wall bookshelves—more of them here but not nearly so nice as the ones Leo built—and wonder aloud at a big fat book whose title is spelled out in angry red Asian characters. What's that? I ask Sabrina. Oh, she says, with the air of someone who's had it explained to her before, that's Solzhenitsyn's *August 1914: Red Wheel*, but in

Malaysian. I suddenly understand what's wrong with this picture: I'm reading about the Borscht Belt in the middle of the Gulag. No wonder I can't retain my focus.

Part of the appeal of books, of course, is that they're the cheapest and easiest way to transport you from the world you know into one you don't. That's why people who'd never leave the house read travel tomes and why, on a swelteringly hot summer day, you can have fun with, say, *Smilla's Sense of Snow*. A friend of mine tells me that he likes to listen to tapes of Trollope novels while negotiating New York City traffic because he likes the clash of his inner and outer worlds: "The lovely British voice on the tape is saying, 'And the vicar went into the parish,' just as I'm yelling in my best New Yorkese, 'Hey, Buddy, up yours!' to the cabdriver on my right." Reading's ability to beam you up to a different world is a good part of the reason people like me do it in the first place—because dollar for dollar, hour per hour, it's the most expedient way to get from our proscribed little "here" to an imagined, intriguing "there." Part time machine, part Concorde, part ejector seat, books are our salvation.

But here I am in rural, outer Vermont, having traveled this time by train, not page. And suddenly, *Funnymen*—a book that back in New York might well have transported me happily to the Catskills—seems superfluous. I was already in a new world. Besides, reading a novel about comedians here seemed somehow inappropriate, sort of like giggling over *Bridget Jones's Diary* at a divorce proceeding. There was no way I was going to get through it.

So I started prowling Solzhenitsyn's shelves. "Why not try

something by the great man himself?" my exasperated husband suggests. But by now my college-major Spanish is so rusty I can barely understand what my building superintendent says, let alone the thoughts of the great writer. And I don't read Russian—or Croat or Chinese or Malaysian for that matter—so my options are limited. In fact, in both of these houses, except for a dog-eared copy of *Gulliver's Travels* I find in one of the sons' bedrooms upstairs, there's almost nothing that's both (a) in English and (b) not about or by Solzhenitsyn himself. For a brief moment, I consider *One Day in the Life of Ivan Denisovich*, which I remember vaguely from a college world history course, but then I remember the only reason I read it then: some Russian novel was required, and *Ivan Denisovich* was the shortest one on the list. Eventually, I uncover a copy of a book in English called *Solzhenitsyn: Soul in Exile*, which I gather is one of the few biographies sanctioned by the Solzhenitsyn family, as there is a boxful of them standing by the door. It's a book I never, ever would have read under any other circumstances, but I'm in Russia now, I tell myself. I need to do as the Russians do. What's more: I'm grateful to have a window on the world I've just entered.

Remember how I said I expected to learn some lessons about reading? Well, I just never thought they'd be so prosaic—or would come so soon. But by the time Leo and Charley and I were settled back onto the train to New York, I'd figured out a few things. To wit: (1) Choosing a book is not all that different from choosing a house. There are really only three rules: location, location, and location. And (2) In reading, as in life, even if you know what you're doing, you really kind of don't. To paraphrase the old saw: If you want to make the book god laugh, show him your reading list.

"How do you choose your books?" my friends had asked. Less than a week into my project, I can now tell them the beginning of the truth. I don't always choose the books, I'll say. Sometimes the books choose me.

January 20

A Word About Leo

ere's a snapshot of Leo's and my bedroom. On my side, the right side, of the bed, is a table heaped with books and magazines and stray papers and catalogues and old bank receipts and who knows what else. On Leo's side, on an identical table, are: two neatly lined-up copies of food magazines, a couple of cookbooks, and a hardcover copy of Caleb Carr's *Killing Time* that has been sitting there, unopened, for about a year. You could be in the first week of Psychology 101 to figure out what this means: I'm a compulsive slob while Leo's a compulsive neatnik; Leo wouldn't shop by catalogue if his life depended on it, and his idea of aspirational literature almost always involves food.

To me, it shows simply that I am a card-carrying member of the compulsive readers' society. He, on the other hand, is not.

It's a truism of conventional therapeutic thinking that when choosing a mate, most people try to re-create or react against a relationship they had in childhood. Most often, it seems women set out to marry men like their fathers or precisely the opposite of their fathers, men look for or run from their mothers, and so on and so on.

In my case, I married my brother.

Like Leo, my younger brother Jon is now in the design business: he is a licensed architect and for several years designed furniture. As a kid, he was a whiz at mechanics and spatial relations. If I was a dutiful good student, Jon cared less about school than about going around the neighborhood and getting old ladies to give him their broken toasters so that he could charge them a dollar to fix them. Why bother with other people's worlds made of words? was his philosophy. He'd always rather build another Go-Kart.

Jon was something of an oddity in our family, where "Look it up" was the answer to most questions and where, for a period of a few years while I was in elementary school, my mother regularly brought the dictionary to the dinner table. But weird as he was in our particular household constellation, he was my little brother, and he was familiar. We made plenty of fun of him, that's for sure, but ultimately he provided me a great service. Because of Jon, I grew up knowing that nonreaders could be people, too.

So when I met Leo, the fact that he had almost never read a book for pleasure didn't strike me as all that important. First of all, we had many other surface differences to contend with: He's one of eleven children born to Japanese-American parents in a working-class neighborhood in Chicago; I'm the privileged daughter of East Coast professionals. He grew up Catholic (thanks to his parents' conversion in the detention camps during WWII); I'm a secularized Jew. He's quiet; I can't shut up. That we had different interests—his spatial, mine verbal—was the least of it.

Which is not to say that it's easy living with someone who has no feeling at all about the very things about which I am so passionate: books, the people who write them, and those who read them. (Relationship fact #1: The very thing that attracted you to your partner will become the thing that drives you nuts.) It's true that I often become frustrated when he doesn't get my references. And I'm sure it's no picnic for him to have a wife who not only floods his bedroom with paper but regularly spends hours on the phone dissecting the novel of the moment and then begs off going to the movies or out to dinner so she can "get some reading done." But to his credit—and in defiance of relationship fact #2: Despite what you say, you're always trying to change your partner—he doesn't gripe much about it. In fact, he views my reading habit as an acceptable, if not completely interesting, quirk. I recently overheard him telling a friend, almost pridefully, that his wife has read "every book in the universe."

I, on the other hand, fully subscribe to relationship fact #2, and am constantly trying to interest him in this or that book I've discovered. Here, for example, is a partial list of the books (other than the aforementioned Caleb Carr title) I've left on his pillow over the years:

James Ellroy's *My Dark Places* (because he asked for it)
Henry Dunow's *The Way Home* (because it's about baseball
    and baseball is a sport, I think, and Leo likes sports)

Lee Hill's *A Grand Guy: The Art and Life of Terry Southern* (because Leo knew the gonzo writer through *SNL* and when we happened to meet him one night at a reunion party, even Leo, who is famously blasé, became visibly excited)

Several books by Patrick O'Brian (because Leo has developed a magnificent midlife obsession with sailing)

Mario Puzo's *Omerta* (because somebody gave it to me. Who knows why?)

As far as I know, he hasn't read any of them.

It's annoying to have your recommendations ignored, but the minor pique I feel most of the time is exacerbated mightily by his refusal to read any of the books I've shelved in the library under an invisible but still very real category. These are the novels and stories and nonfiction accounts of Asian-American experience, of "mixed" marriage, of biracial children, books like Don Lee's *Yellow*, David Wong Louie's *The Barbarians Are Coming*, Shawn Wong's *American Knees*. Again, despite my urging, Leo hasn't read any of them. But I have read them all.

I worry sometimes that it's shallow to want to read about your own life and your own world all the time, but there's always something pleasing and comforting about coming across a character or a situation you think you already know; it's a validation of your own experience. That I should feel some draw, even now, to a book like *Marjorie Morningstar* isn't surprising. But had I not married Leo and had Charley, I doubt I would have developed such an interest in reading about what the Japanese-American internment camps were like, or how complicated it is, even now in multi-culti America, to not be white. Like every wife or husband, but especially one who sees her partner's backstory as more important to preserve than her own, I find his topics have become mine.

My first introduction to this literary subcategory took place about ten years ago, soon after Leo and I were married. An editor from a weekly consumer magazine invited me up to his offices to paw through stacks of proofs and choose some books for review. This came after months of my begging him for work, and a hazing period during which he assigned me reviews of self-help titles and exercise books—and I was clearly thrilled. I remember going into the book room at the magazine—a room at least twice the size of my library today—and feeling less overwhelmed than exhilarated by all the possibilities there. "Take two to start," he told me. Only two? I emerged, an hour later, with these galleys: *The Beauty Myth*, by Naomi Wolf, and something I'd never heard of, but whose title intrigued me for obvious reasons: a memoir called *Turning Japanese*, by a writer named David Mura.

I started with *The Beauty Myth* (read about what you know!) but didn't get too far; I remember thinking that everything Wolf said in her book about how our culture makes women neurotic about their appearance—duh!—had been more wisely and wittily dissected at the average dinner party. But once I sat down with *Turning Japanese*, I was hooked. The memoir of a second-generation Japanese-American married to a Caucasian woman but searching for his roots immediately struck a chord. Like Leo, Mura was an artist—a poet. He grew up, like Leo, in Chicago, and he was about Leo's age. Mura's family had "assimilated" to the point of shortening their name from Uyemura; Leo is called Leo, but his real name in his family is Akira. Thanks to an artist grant, Mura took his family to Japan for a year, half-expecting that a return to the land of his ancestry would provide him with the sense of belonging he'd never quite felt in the States. (Leo, at this point, had never been to Japan either, but he held it out in his mind as something of the promised land.) The trip wasn't altogether satisfying, because the notoriously xenophobic Japanese-born Japanese considered him a foreigner—he was "other" even there—but along the way, he did come face to face with some of his own confusions and prejudices, some of which had to do with his wife. I remember that the review I eventually wrote focused on that wife, and on the fact that Mura seemed remarkably unsympathetic to her discomfort during that year. Not only did she live through his flirtation with another woman, but as a tall, big-boned woman (read about what you know!), she regularly felt frustrated by the inability to find clothes or shoes in her size.

I became obsessed enough with *Turning Japanese* back then that I immediately went out and bought several copies, which I gave as gifts to my Yoshimura nieces and nephews that Christmas. But Leo never read it, and I moved on. But recently I discovered Mura's subsequent book, *Where the Body Meets Memory*. And this time I've been torturing Leo about it.

Where the Body Meets Memory is a pretentious title for a book that, in its first half, at least, is a moving rumination on growing up Japanese-American right after WWII. (It then, unfortunately, devolves into an account of Mura's premarital sexaholism—always with white women, of course—that more properly belongs on an episode of *The Jerry Springer Show* than in a literary memoir.) It describes the way Mura struggled with his parents, who, like Leo's, almost never talked about their experiences in the camps, except in the most benign ways. (The Yoshimuras, who were interned at Manzanar near Santa Ana, California, always refer to this time as their years "at camp," as if they'd been shuffleboarding in the Adirondacks.) Mura discusses the fact that his sister—and several other Japanese-American women he knows—almost never dated Asian men because it felt "too incestuous." (In Leo's family, only one of his ten siblings is married to another Asian, and Leo has never even dated one.)

On page after page, I underlined passages. There was the revelation that in the camps, his parents decided they'd need to be two hundred percent American from then on; in Leo's family, the line was "Be more American than the Americans." At one point, Mura complains to his wife that his father talks about the camps "as if they were nothing." My father-in-law regularly sidesteps any questions Leo or I pose about that period with the disclaimer: "Compared to what the Germans did to the Jews [pointed reference to me, here], it was nothing." By the time I reached page 45, I was so agitated and the book was so marked up that I called Leo at the studio.

"Listen to this!" I said, as I read him a snippet of conversation between Mura and his father, who, like Leo's father, is a man of few words. "Yeah. So?" came my husband's response.

"It's just like your family!" I nudged.

"Uh-huh," he said.

Maybe another, smarter woman would have let it go at that.

But I couldn't. I went back to the book and called him again, twenty minutes later. "You've got to hear this!" I said. Then I read him this line from Mura: "It's difficult to underestimate how much as a teenager I wanted to fit in, how deeply I assumed a basically white middle-class identity." I'd heard that sentence, almost verbatim, from Leo many times.

"You've got to read this book!" I exhorted.

I heard the sharp intake of breath that I knew meant he was getting fed up with me. "Sara, will you just leave me alone?" he said.

And then he said something that flies in the face of everything I thought I knew about reading, something that destroyed my whole theory of reading about what you know.

"Why should I read it?" he said. "I don't need to. I lived it."

Double-Booked

When you think and talk about books as much as I do, sooner or later you hear just about every theory. Never read in bed, some say; others say that's the only place. Always read the book before you see the movie, they'll tell you—except others will tell you the opposite. Or this, from a guy I dated when I first came to New York: "Always have a couple of things going at once," said Ray—a writer, natch!—once he'd gotten a load of my library habit. "That way," he said, "you'll never be lonely."

Ray was wrong about a lot of things, but about that, at least, he was right. By double-booking—keeping one book at home and another in my backpack or glove compartment—I always had something to do while stuck in traffic, stranded in a long line, or as it turned out, sitting by the phone waiting for him to call.

He's now long gone, but the double-booking habit has remained.

I started this week with *Nine Parts of Desire*, Geraldine Brooks's collection of essays about her interaction with Islamic women in the mid-1990s. While well reviewed when it was first published, it did not exactly change the configuration of the bestseller lists, maybe because of its unfortunate timing. It came out in 1995, at just about the moment that the locus of attention for most Americans was switching from the Middle East to the NASDAQ. But my sister Liza told me she'd liked it, and even gave me the copy she'd bought at a secondhand bookstore near the Georgia farm where she lives. It still had the Newnan bookshop sticker on it.

When I get a book, or a recommendation of a book, from Liza, I take it seriously because as a novelist (*Playing Botticelli*) and a reviewer, she's highly critical of most contemporary work and her praise comes so infrequently. (I think of her as the kid, Mikey, from the old cereal commercial, the one in which the little boy rejects every breakfast suggestion except one. "Mikey likes it! He likes it!" the other kids crow in amazement.) I'm particularly susceptible to Liza's suggestions because, as my big sister (she's six years older), she holds the position, for better and worse, as my intellectual mentor. It was because of Liza that I, who was born at the tail end of the baby boom, became a full-fledged Bob Dylan freak, able to chant all the words to Dylan's obscure "Motorpsycho Nightmare" on the school bus when I was in seventh grade. It was because of Liza that I first heard of Jane Austen. (The paperback of *Northanger Abbey* that sits on my shelf today has her name in it.) It's because of Liza that I began to develop whatever social conscience I now have. (The first book she gave me, when I was about twelve, was a photojournalistic essay about a tenement. Her inscription read: "Read This and Think of Our Back Yard.") Although we didn't always get along so well—she's laughing now, if she's reading this, because of the enormity of that understatement—I always wanted to be like her, especially in the brainy department.

We joke sometimes that as two middle-aged writers, we've become like the best friends in the old George Cukor movie *Rich and Famous:* she's the brilliant but broke poet played by Jacqueline Bisset; but for some substantial physical differences, I'm the Candice Bergen character, more concerned with the commerce of book publishing than with art. And it's true: While Liza has spent most of her adult life writing serious fiction, I've been writing about fiction, serious and not. She's "high" culture, I'm "low." While she may envy my more active, public life, I'm always more than a little jealous of her creative talent—and so the balance is maintained. As long as our particular twains never meet, we do fine.

But because of our role-playing history, sometimes her recommendations scare me. Ever the little sister, I wonder if I'll be "up to" whatever book or concept she recommends. Which probably explains why I'd filed *Nine Parts of Desire* high up on the shelf, where I could conveniently "forget" about it. But now, with yet another war raging in the Middle East, and a new paperback edition in the bookstores, I summoned Liza's gift down. I was relieved to find the collection of essays about women chafing, surviving, and very rarely thriving in Muslim countries both erudite and immensely readable. It was also a book I could take out in public.

While we rarely admit it, what we read speaks, well, volumes about us. I remember, several years ago, coming upon a profile of Sandy Hill Pittman, then the wife of MTV cofounder and now deposed AOL Time Warner COO Bob Pittman. Apparently, they met on an airplane, back in the days when Sandy worked at a fashion magazine. Spying the attractive Bob sitting near her, she made a calculated decision—to be seen reading *The New Yorker* instead of, say, *Mademoiselle.* The clip is lost to me now, but I remember her being quoted as saying, quite bluntly and unapologetically, that she wanted this cute guy to think she was the kind of person who read something serious and worthy. P.S. Her scam worked, at least temporarily; the two married and had a son, though they're now divorced and Pittman is married to someone else, about whose reading habits little is known.

I'd like to think I'm above this kind of ruse—and besides, Leo is the type who could tell you what I was wearing on our first date, fourteen years ago (hint: there's a hat involved) faster than what I read in bed last night—but the truth is, a book can be a good conversation (and relationship) starter. In college, I always went for the dark, poetic types who carried around a slim volume of T. S. Eliot in their back jeans pocket. Whether they actually read the books or not didn't matter: their choice of reading material defined them and attracted me. People notice what you read and judge you by it. Which is why if I were going to read Danielle Steel, I wouldn't do it at the office. But *Nine Parts of Desire* speaks to anyone who might be listening: I'm smart, it says. I'm concerned with current events, it announces. I am a serious person.

And I am a serious person, sometimes, but I also like my share of fun. So when my old friend Robin slipped me an advance copy of *Her,* the third book by former publishing executive Laura Zigman, I abandoned *Nine Parts* in what they call one New York minute. Zigman made something of a splash a few years back with *Animal Husbandry,* a light, single-woman-looking-for-love novel. (The book was also the basis for an Ashley Judd vehicle called *Someone Like You,* which left the theaters in about as much time as it took most of us to read the far more charming novel.) It was gimmicky, but in those pre–Bridget Jones days, it seemed fresh. And I loved it. So on the night of our dinner, I returned home a little buzzed and immediately gulped down the first adorable chapters of *Her,* which promised to be a delightful novel about a woman so obsessed with her fiancé's ex that she just about kills her relationship. *Her,* I decided, would be my bedtime reading. *Nine Parts* would go with me out of the house.

But it's not only because *Nine Parts* has better show-off potential that it got the exalted place in my Maria Turgeon handbag. A book of discrete essays, it is better suited to the stop-and-start nature of my daytime reading (on the bus; in between answering Charley's questions on his homework; in a restaurant waiting for a tardy lunch date). It's also paperback, which makes it easier to carry around than the brand-new hardcover *Her.* Hardcovers have jackets, and I've learned the hard way that those jackets are not meant to survive the constant push-and-pull of the here-and-there reader. They get ripped, and beat-up, and pretty soon you've got a $25 piece of literature that looks like it's covered in a paper dishrag. A few times, I thought to remove the jackets entirely and just carry the actual book. But somehow the covers never find the books again—last week I found the cover to *The Ash Garden*, which I read months ago, in a dust pile at the back of my closet. As surely as the dryer invariably turns up single socks, bookless jackets disappear.

But isn't it weird, a friend asks, to divide your concentration between something so grave as the sorry state of womanhood abroad and the admittedly flimsy story of a privileged D.C. fiancée with too much time on her hands? On the contrary. With stories so different, you're in virtually no danger of conflating the two and wondering why, say, Zigman's Elise doesn't wear a *hijab* to stalk her nemesis. Likewise, you're surely not going to expect Brooks's Western-educated assistant—who becomes an Islamic extremist— to admit she's jealous that her fiancé's ex is thinner than she. It may be true that this is a particularly unusual reading cocktail I've mixed up, but for me, at least, it works.

Woody Allen once said that the advantage of bisexuality is that it doubles your chances of finding a date on Saturday night. Having a bifurcated reading brain—one part that likes "junk" and one that reveres "literature"—is the same kind of satisfying. You don't have to be any one thing and you don't have to think any one way. And should you happen upon different kinds of people in different situations, your pool of conversation topics is twice as deep.

Anyway, I've started to think that the books I've been reading this week aren't as different as they at first appear. Brooks's work, while educational, also offers us Westerners a frisson of gratitude that however bad or problematic or troublesome our superficial lives may be, we're still better off than our sisters toiling (or in most cases, not even being allowed to toil) under extremist Islamic regimes. Zigman, on the other hand, purports to write about our real lives, or at least the real lives of the thirty-something female book-buying population. But where Brooks is a journalist and recounts events and conversations and beliefs pretty much as they occur, Zigman, a novelist, takes the typical to the extreme. Are unmarried privileged thirty-somethings really as self-involved, however amusingly, as Elise? Of course not. By (over)dramatizing their plight, Zigman allows us the same kind of schadenfreude as Brooks. "No matter what," we can think, "my life isn't *that* bad."

I wouldn't have bothered to explain all this to Liza, as I was pretty sure she'd never heard of, much less read, anything by Laura Zigman, but I figured she'd be pleased to hear I'd gotten to *Nine Parts of Desire*. So I called her. "You were right," I said to flatter my brainy big sister. "This is a terrific book. I'm so glad you gave it to me."

"What book was that again?" she asked.

I told her.

"I didn't give that to you," she said. "I don't know a thing about it."

I was suddenly the eight-year-old who had brought her the wrong treat from the Dairy Queen on the corner. "But it has a Newnan bookshop sticker on it!" I almost wailed.

"Well," she replied, sounding, I thought, like the fourteen-year-old who'd been purposely vague about what treat she wanted me to fetch her in the first place, "I'm usually reading a couple of things at once, so maybe I just don't remember."

Liza recommended Kate Manning's *Whitegirl*, too, and this time I'd be shocked if she didn't remember. She'd liked it so much she had placed a specific call to tell me about it last fall and offered to give me the bound manuscript she'd read for review purposes when we got together at Christmas. Now, three months later—and three hundred miles away—it remained at the bottom of the bedside pile. (A truth: Sometimes that pile is arranged by size—so bound manuscripts would naturally go on the bottom—instead of by my degree of interest.) But as I pack for my five-day vacation in Florida to visit my mother, I decide to take a look at it.

It's been only a couple of weeks since my *Funnymen* debacle, so I want to be careful. I want to take something that won't be too jarring in the new world, but I also need it to be something that will keep me from mouthing off at my mother during the day and keep me company on the nights when Mom has gone to bed at eight P.M. and my very few friends there are out of town. When I talked to Liza the night before I left, she reminded me of *White-girl*. I hung up and dug out the manuscript, which bore a striking resemblance to—and sparked a memory of—a book I'd taken on my annual Mom visit a few years earlier. On that trip, I'd spent a long layover in the Miami airport reading most of Kurt Andersen's *Turn of the Century*—also a very long book, also in bound manuscript—and laughing out loud so many times that the woman sitting next to me finally asked what the book was that was obviously making me so happy. Call me superstitious, but this seemed a good omen for *Whitegirl:* now all I had to do was get far enough in to be sure it would retain my interest.

When Liza handed over the hulking mass of pages covered in blue plastic, she hadn't said much about it, beyond that she thought I'd relate. The story of a white model married to a black athlete, it raised some of the kinds of questions Liza and I have often discussed about my own interracial marriage. While Leo is not famous, or nearly as rich, as the character in the book, who was a champion skier, then a sports commentator, and finally a movie star, our relationship has a lot in common with the one Manning writes about. I was immediately impressed by how she managed to show, for example, that despite the greater acceptance of race and multiculturalism and blah blah blah, such "mixed marriages" had specific issues of their own.

Before anybody who's read *Whitegirl* worries that they should call 911 on my behalf, I should say that the plot of the novel does not mimic my life. Manning's narrative opens with Charlotte, the now ex-model and mother, reeling from a violent attack that may or may not have been perpetrated by her estranged husband. It then proceeds to flash back through the many years of Charlotte and Milo's relationship, from their first meeting in college through their next encounter in New York, through the birth of their children, through Charlotte's unfortunate encounter with a scandal-hungry press, up to the attack and the potential dissolution of their marriage. Still, there are vignettes that I found strangely familiar, as when Charlotte confesses to her feelings about being the only white person in a room: it reminded me of walking into Leo's parents' house for our first Christmas together and feeling, for the first time, completely "other." ("That's how I've felt most of my life," Leo told me when we talked about it later.) And while Leo's temper is nowhere near as explosive as Milo's, there is a rage in him that when analyzed, usually comes down, like Milo's, to his lifelong sense of, as he puts it, not being able to be mistaken for Cary Grant.

It's impossible to miss the O. J. Simpson–like overtones to the plot in *Whitegirl*, but still, to dismiss it as a cheesy roman à clef is to miss the subtle way in which Manning—who is white and who, as far as I know, has always been married to a white lawyer—understands how race pervades every aspect of a relationship, at least as much for the "majority" partner as for the minority one. Even when the couple is famous and rich—or maybe because Charlotte and Milo are famous and rich—their every problem is underwritten by race, a situation that seemed very familiar to me. The major criticism of the book has been that Charlotte comes off as too much of a cipher, a nonperson—and that she's stupid. And while I admit that I heard a false note when Charlotte confuses Goldman Sachs, the investment bank, with Saks Fifth Avenue, the department store—no one could be that dumb, not even a model!—her lack of distinctive personality is, in a way, the point. When your own story is so benign compared with that of someone whose ancestors were slaves, or interned in detention camps, even, it's easy to be swallowed up in his story at the expense of your own.

I hadn't figured all this out that pre-vacation night, of course. All I knew then was that I needed to get a couple of chapters under my belt, the better to ensure I wouldn't end up on the plane with a book I hated and, thus, with nothing to read. At ten o'clock, with Charley safely in bed, I sat down to read a bit. Except that I couldn't put the manuscript down after Chapter 3. Or Chapter 5. Or Chapter 10, for that matter. It was two, then three, then four in the morning as I lay on the living room couch, awkwardly manipulating the bulky manuscript bound in plastic and punctuated by spindles up the side, like the kind we used to use in high school. I was so enthralled that I barely noticed the paper cuts and back strain. There's no other way to say it: I fell in love.

Explaining the moment of connection between a reader and a book to someone who's never experienced it is like trying to describe sex to a virgin. A friend of mine says that when he meets a book he loves, he starts to shake involuntarily. For me, the feeling comes in a rush: I'm reading along and suddenly a word or phrase or scene enlarges before my eyes and soon everything around me is just so much fuzzy background. The phone can ring, the toast can burn, the child can call out, but to me, they're all in a distant dream. The book—this beautiful creature in my hands!—is everything I've ever wanted, as unexpected and inevitable as love.

Where did it come from? How did I live without it for so long? I have to read and read and read, all the while knowing that the more aggressively I pursue my passion, the sooner it will end and then I will be bereft. A young boy I know felt that way about *Harry Potter and the Goblet of Fire*; having finished it in a sixteen-hour marathon, he wandered his house in something approximating despair. Book lovers simply have no choice: we can't tear ourselves away from the beloved.

And oh, the things I've done for love. I've lied ("No, honey, I got tied up at the office," when in fact I was staying late to squeeze in a few more pages); cheated (skipped gym class in favor of the at-home StairMaster, which is not only an easier workout but one that lets you read as you sweat); and stolen (once, having mistakenly left my book at home, I ducked into a bookstore to read a couple of chapters for free). Even sacred family rituals are fair game: I recently heard about a woman who instituted a weekly Soup Night because she figured out that she could stand at the stove all afternoon, stirring with one hand and turning pages of the latest Mary Higgins Clark with the other.

Who will be hit with the thunderbolt, and during which book, and why, is as magical as love itself, and probably as unanalyzable. It's predictable that I'd fall for, say, David Gilmour's *How Boys See Girls*, a Canadian novel about a down-and-out journalist who reminded me of any number of people I know—my *aha* moment in that book came when Gilmour described a character's eating style as "turning [food] over in his maw like laundry in a dryer"—but who knew I'd be so crazy for Ron Hansen's *Atticus* that I'd be sneaking glances at it, hidden under my notebook, during a business meeting? Like those stories in women's magazines that ask you to guess which man looks as though he goes with which woman, how books and people mate remains, forever, a mystery.

That said, it's not surprising that I knew, pretty early on, that *Whitegirl* and I would have a future together; there was Liza's recommendation, and the interracial marriage at its core. But I didn't really know it would take hold the way it did, until I started reading that night, and arrived, on page 11, at Charlotte's first glimpse of Milo, in which she unabashedly remarked, "Strange, to see a black man carrying skis." Wow, I thought, Kate Manning's going to take some flak from the PC police for that! It was the first of many times in this otherwise traditional "women's novel" that I was stopped short by the author's bravery.

Whitegirl is not a perfect novel, of course. The central question—did Milo attack and disfigure Charlotte, or was it someone else?—is a little hokey, and there are those moments when Charlotte seems too dumb to be true. But Manning's ancillary characters, like Milo's sister, who educates Charlotte in the ways of the Robicheaux family, and Darryl Haines, the friend who openly disapproves of Milo's marriage to a white woman, are great. So, too, is the way Manning conveys the walk-on-eggs quality of Charlotte's choices and the chauvinism that lives on both sides of the racial divide. This novel was more than I expected, and the perfect choice of an intelligent, consuming novel to take on vacation.

Except that *Whitegirl* never got to Key West with me that day. By the time I had to leave for the airport, I'd slept for three hours and had about fifty pages of the manuscript left to read. What to do? It clearly wasn't worth lugging the whole thing now, but it was too late to decide on a proper substitute. Besides, I couldn't leave *Whitegirl* at home anyway. Cannot separate from the beloved, remember? Instead, I did something I never would have done with a published book, or even a galley: I ripped open the plastic cover, removed the remaining pages from the spindles, and tucked them in my bag.

Those, of course, I read in the cab to the airport.

And that's how I ended up wandering to the gate, feeling like that ninth-grader who'd just finished Harry Potter. I looked plaintively at the rack of paperbacks at the newsstand. *Could it be you?* I'd think as I fondled *The Blind Assassin. Could you be my next true love?* But I wasn't getting the vibe. I finally gave up, bought a couple of magazines, and boarded the plane, looking for all the world like a person who'd just lost her best friend. Which, of course, for that day at least, I had.

February 13

92 in the Shade

To arrive in Key West bookless is only slightly less jarring than finding oneself hatless in Dallas. A famously literary community—Hemingway lived (and drank) here, as have authors from Annie Dillard to Thomas McGuane to Edmund White—it has a year-round population of just over 35,000 people but supports half a dozen independent bookstores. Only in Key West can you go from a small bookstore signing for Ann Beattie to a poolside paperback Grisham festival: it's that kind of bilevel, bifurcated place.

Key West would be the perfect place to double-book, in fact, because tastes here run from the highest of the highbrow (Michael Ondaatje, who's a regular visitor) to the lowest of the low (I see lots of Signet romances at the beach). But I've blown it this time: with *Whitegirl* finished, I'm not even prepared to uni-book.

I'm also going to be alone with Mom for a few days.

There was a popular TV show in the mid-1980s called *thirty-*

something that I generally found treacly and embarrassing. But I remember it fondly because of one particular scene that came early in the show's run. Two women friends are talking—I think their names were Hope and Ellen—about an impending visit from one of their mothers. "I love my mother, I really do," the soon-to-be-visited one says. "So how come after ten minutes I want to kill somebody?"

"Ten minutes?" her friend replies. "What's your secret?"

There's nothing wrong with my mother; in fact, I think she's a great woman, having lived eighty-four years, raised four of the not-easiest children in the world, and managed, defying the suspicions of those ungrateful children, to create a full life for herself after my father died twelve years ago. In her "dotage," as she calls it, she has refashioned herself into a poet and now gives readings around town. She has lots of friends, enjoys living alone, and is, for the most part, uncomplaining and grateful to have the money and good health to live as she does. We talk on the phone several times a week, just kibitzing, as she'd say; when I was little, she'd routinely predict that I'd be the joy of her old age and I hope and believe that in some ways that has been true.

So why, after one evening in her company, do I start to feel like one of those women on *thirtysomething*? Maybe we know each other too well. Between the continual criticism—"Get your hair out of your eyes!" she says repeatedly, proving once and for all that certain remarks don't lose power after adolescence—and the relentless observation and discussion of her, my, and everybody else's weight, I start feeling nasty.

What I want to say: "Oh, will you please just shut up!"

What I do say: "So Mom, got anything good to read?"

I may have come late to passionate reading, but I caught on pretty early that a book can be the perfect shield against potentially piercing situations. Not only is reading a distraction during difficult times—whether they be sitting in the waiting room at the lab while the technicians and doctors are conferring about your mammogram or, yes, spending a few unchaperoned days with a well-meaning but colossally annoying parent—but it's a highly socially respectable means of social avoidance. You can't tell an obnoxious seatmate on a plane, for example, that his obstreperous pontificating about the virtues of saccharin over NutraSweet is driving you batty, but you can tell him you're in the middle of *A Tale of Two Cities* and you simply must get back to it. He may think you boringly bookish, but if you do it right, he probably can't call you rude.

There are people who take their socially protective reading to an extreme, of course, like a woman I used to know who would regularly bring novels to cocktail parties and sit in the corner turning pages while everybody else milled around her. (I say "used to" because after a while I stopped inviting her to my house.) But I can understand why she did it. Especially for people whose daily lives and jobs and worlds require them to interact with other humans all day, a book can be a savior. A book is a way to shut out the noise of the world. It's a way to be alone without being totally alone.

Growing up in the middle of four kids and two parents of various degrees of rambunctiousness, I learned two life lessons: (1) You have to talk loud to be heard, and if you can develop a sense of humor and insert it into much of what you say, you'll be heard even better. And (2) You need escape. You need a place to go—actual or mental—where no one can bother you, where your sports-loving older brother and his noisy friends can't reach you, where your sister's superiority can't touch you, where your sweet but annoying little brother can't embarrass you. When I talk to Leo about his childhood household—which, with ten siblings, was only about five hundred times (these things are exponential) more chaotic than mine—he tells me he used to retire regularly to a closet to draw and paint pictures of himself as a "dog in space": a little kid with glasses shut up in a soundproof capsule. A place, in other words, where nobody would get to him.

My situation was a lot less dramatic, and as I've said, I wasn't one of those kids who never learned to ride a bike because I was in-tent on finishing the complete works of J. R. R. Tolkien by the time I was ten. But I knew early how to protect myself from too much attention and unwanted noise: tell Mom and Dad you had to read a book. Not only did it please them—"My daughter, the reader!"—but it got them off my back. Never mind that my mother would often come in the next hour or day and ask for a mini book report; at least for the moment I needed it, I could get away.

So here, in my mother's apartment, I had hit on the exact right means of escape from conversation about my brother Jon's recent bad run in the market and Charley's worrisome appetite for candy. A frustrated writer throughout much of her life, my mother has always positioned herself in her group of friends as the intel-lectual, and the reader, and she does, in fact, have quite a col-lection of what, in the thirties, forties, and fifties, was important contemporary literature. She collected the works of Hemingway, for example, and prides herself on some rare pieces: a first edition with the cover of *For Whom the Bell Tolls* that, when you open it, turns out to be the text of *A Farewell to Arms*. And she loves to talk about her experiences with certain writers and their books (clearly, some things are genetic). I couldn't begin to tell you how many times I've heard the stories of her brief correspondence with Philip Roth and about the time, most famously in our family, that she goaded my father to follow Hemingway into a bar's men's room in Cuba in the fifties to catch him off guard and get him to sign her (anatomically correct) copy of *The Sun Also Rises*.

But what would I pick? Fresh from *Whitegirl*, I was still harboring the illusion that I could fall madly in love all over again with something I'd never considered before. But a quick root through June's shelves suggested I'd have trouble being surprised by anything here; I already knew most of these books. Usually, I love browsing in someone else's life, especially if it's a stranger's, because you can tell so much about a person by the kind of books they read. A few years ago, when Leo and Charley and I began to rent a house at the beach in the summer, I compiled an impression of the owner, whom I'd never met, based on the titles she stocked. All I knew about her, going in, was that she was an older woman who'd once been married to a well-known TV producer, so I wasn't surprised to find a complete collection of anchorman Tom Brokaw's work. But the fact that she also had, on the top of the pile on the coffee table, the memoir *Leading with My Heart*, by Bill Clinton's mother, Virginia Kelley, told me she was probably sprightly and mouthy and not all that conventional. And I loved her, sight unseen, for her copy of one of my favorite books—*The Spirit Catches You and You Fall Down*, by Anne Fadiman; not only was it there on the shelf, but it was obviously well thumbed and there were a lot of pages with the corners turned down.

But what my mother had done, for the most part, was transplant the books from our Pennsylvania home to this apartment, when my parents moved here in 1984. There were the Jackie Collins and Harold Robbins novels that she must have unearthed from under my adolescent bed, the few books my father—like Leo, not much of a reader; how Freudian is that?—read for pleasure, and of course much of the Hemingwayana, including A. E. Hotchner's *Papa Hemingway*, which June regularly quoted from back in the day. One of my mother's and my favorite pieces of family lore is the fact that, as a kid, I looked so much like her that even a blind stranger in a crowded theater would be able to pick me out as "June Nelson's daughter." That's the way I felt going through her shelves. Even if I'd never been to this apartment before, and had never been told who lived here, I'd know in seconds that it was June's house just by looking through the shelves. They tell her whole life's story.

And, of course, a good portion of mine. Remember how I said I fell in love with *Marjorie Morningstar* when my mother gave it to me as an adolescent? Well, here it is, in all its tattered 1950s glory, on a shelf under her living room TV. Just picking it up takes me back thirty years. I remember her handing it to me and me going off into my overdecorated (with pink flowers, no less) suburban bedroom and staying up all night to read it. By morning, I was at my mother's door—and crying. "Why didn't she marry him?" I cried, referring to Marjorie's ultimate decision not to run off with her prince charming, Noel Airman, a songwriter whom the adults had deemed not right for her because he (a) didn't have any money and (b) was a self-loathing Jew who'd changed his name from Ehrmann (and taken "Noel," which means Christmas, for God's sake) and sneered openly at Jewish middle-class life. "I don't get it."

June's reaction is lost to history, but if I had to guess, I'd say she probably wasn't pleased. Of all the books she could have given me—and soon did—books like *A Bell for Adano* and *A Farewell to Arms* and *Of Human Bondage*, she had chosen this one. Looking back, I can see why: We were an aspiring Jewish family in a rapidly assimilating world. I was becoming a rebellious daughter who regularly hung out with kids from outside the proscribed community—which meant, in those innocent times, boys who went to public school, weren't Jewish (Brett Friedman had long given way to someone named Dugan), and were, by her lights, "wild." If I was not so pretty and nowhere near as self-assured as La Morningstar (as she called herself; the family name was Morgenstern), like her I wanted to be an actress, swore I'd never again live in the suburbs, and most important of all, believed that love should conquer all. My despair at what I saw as Marjorie's "selling out"—marrying an unglamorous Jewish lawyer and moving to Scarsdale—could not have made June happy.

I've thought a lot about *Marjorie Morningstar* in the intervening decades. I remembered it as the ultimate book about growing up, about good-girl rebellion, about pursuing your dreams. Most of all, I thought of it as a grand love story—or as the jacket copy on the beat-up edition I held in my hand put it: "An intimate picture of a girl growing into womanhood through the stresses of passion." (Don't you love that fifties-speak?)

"Maybe I'll reread this?" I say to June now.

She just laughs. "Again?" she says.

It's always dangerous to reread the pivotal books of your youth. Like discovering poetry or journals you wrote as a teenager, revisiting your adolescent feelings about books can be at best embarrassing and often excruciating. I still cringe, for example, when I remember my response to *Zelda*, which is the second grown-up book June ever gave me. I was so captivated by Nancy Milford's portrait of F. Scott Fitgerald's doomed wife and so convinced that poor Zelda had been a victim of a sexist society that didn't recognize her gifts as a writer that I decided, then and there, to read every scrap of poetry, journalism, and flotsam she ever wrote (luckily, a complete works had been published around the same time) and to boycott Fitzgerald *homme* altogether. That Zelda propelled me to read more of anything is, of course, the good news. And I might still argue that *The Great Gatsby* gets too much praise and attention. But what must my lit professors have thought when, as I was forced by curriculum requirements to read Zelda's husband, my papers veered off into harangues about how Scott wasn't the real writer in the family and that—did you know?—he wasn't such a very nice guy?

So I knew I was taking my youth in my hands to reconnect with Marjorie—and at Mom's, no less—but I was desperate. And curious. Would I end up feeling that I'd scheduled a lunch with an old friend I hadn't seen in years only to discover that five minutes in, I couldn't think of a thing to say and had to get out of there *right now?* If I was lucky, I figured, the worst that would happen was that I'd feel the way I felt when I revisited my old dorm room during a college reunion a couple of years back: Everything was more or less as I remembered it . . . but could it have always been this small?

"I'll report in tomorrow," I tell June.

Sure enough, I was at her door by eight A.M. the next day.

"Did you cry?" she asks.

"Not this time," I tell her. "But it did seem different."

I started reading to her from some scribbled notes:

Then: When Marjorie's father's garment business falls on hard times, the family is forced to give up their Central Park West apartment and move to less tony West End Avenue. This embarrasses the upwardly mobile Marjorie.

Now: When garment businesses—or any businesses, for that matter—go belly-up these days, the CEOs often go to jail, from which West End Avenue is one very far cry. Even if Mr. Morgenstern survived the inevitable SEC probes into his accounting practices, he still probably couldn't afford West End Avenue, where apartments today go for millions. They'd all probably end up in Brooklyn. With roommates.

Then: Marsha Zelenko, Marjorie's poorer, crasser, and fatter best friend off and on throughout her life, is a true original and Marjorie is right in aspiring to be more like her. (Secretly, when I wasn't being Marjorie, I was being Marsha.) But when Marsha "settles" for a nerdy, older businessman, she is revealed to be the pathetic striver Marjorie's parents always said she was. Like Marjorie, I liked her a lot less then.

Now: If they were remaking the movie today, Marsha would be played by Janeane Garofalo (Winona Ryder would probably be Marjorie) and would come off as the standard wisecracking, less attractive best friend we've seen a million times. But she'd become a spokesperson for Weight Watchers, thereby eclipsing Marjorie as a celebrity, and probably end up marrying Noel. I still don't like her, but now it's for different reasons.

Then: The book gets boring toward the end, when Marjorie takes a long boat trip to see Noel in Europe and meets an American guy who is probably working with the Resistance against the Nazis. (Actually, I'm surmising here. I don't remember that part of the book at all; I must have skipped it to get to the love scenes.)

Now: How can Wouk write a 500-page book about Jews in the late 1930s and not even mention the brewing Nazi threat until well past the middle?

But here's the thought that really got June laughing—and I have to say, gave me a bit of pause, too.

Then: Marjorie Morningstar was a talent, a free spirit, and the only thing that held her back was her impossibly uncool parents and their bourgeois values.

Now: Marjorie Morningstar is a self-involved twit who doesn't begin to appreciate the advantages that her long-suffering parents work hard to give her. She could have saved herself a lot of heartbreak if only she'd listened to her mother.

More About Mom

There's a picture that sits on a shelf in my home office that I have always loved, but it has particularly interested me this past week, as I spent hours on my couch there devouring Katharine Graham's *Personal History*. It's a shot of my parents, Charles and June, taken, my mother thinks, outside some European airport, where they'd just landed for a vacation. She can't remember the exact year, but it's clearly the early 1960s, to judge from her Jackie Kennedy–inspired hairstyle and shades and princess coat. My father is characteristically dapper: his shoes match his belt (it's a black-and-white photo, but I wouldn't be at all surprised if both of those were white or, spare me, a kind of canary yellow). He's looking slightly down as he opens his sunglasses with his incredibly long, patrician fingers, and a cigarette hangs from his lips. It was clearly a good time for them, as it was for a lot of Americans: both the family furniture business and their four children were healthy and growing, a young, cool guy was in the

White House, and as my father would surely have said in the imitation hipster-speak he used to borrow from his idol, Frank Sinatra, the world was their oyster.

It's a picture, in other words, of well-fed optimism. There is no hint that in a few years, everything they thought they knew would change. That young, cool guy would be dead, we'd be at war, and every social rule they'd lived by would be de facto repealed. If you'd told my mother then that her daughters would work as hard and make as much money as her sons, or that she might one day have any kind of career herself, she'd have laughed. Though college-educated and reasonably well-to-do, she knew her place: at the country club, at the bridge table, and maybe—just now and then so that she'd always be available to throw dinner parties for my father's business associates—at a continuing-education philosophy course at the local college.

I was thinking about my mother while reading *Personal History*, because it seems to turn on the exact moment I see crystallized in the photo of Charles and June. The mid-sixties were both an end and a beginning for women born in the early part of the twentieth century. It was the moment just before the world turned over for them and their entire generation.

Katharine Graham was born into extraordinary circumstances class-wise, but there was little that differentiated her from other well-born women of the time. The bright daughter of wealthy businessman Eugene Meyer and his wife, Agnes, she went to the tony Madeira School and to Vassar, but in those days, those choices were often more about social pedigree than education. She was expected to—and she did—marry a bright and interesting guy and learn to run a household, raise children, and be a pillar of society. The only unusual thing, early on, was how close she was to her father and how he chose her, not her male siblings, to carry on at *The Washington Post*. But had Eugene not liked Phil as much as he clearly did, even that might not have happened. As with most women of her time, everything that happened to Graham happened because she was somebody's daughter and/or somebody's wife.

But then the whole production derailed when Phil, who'd been spiraling into mental illness for years, committed suicide at the family's weekend home in the country. Suddenly, Katharine Graham had two choices: she could sell the company her father had built for her, or she could, as they used to say in those days, roll up her sleeves and go to work. Though she had virtually no real experience of the newspaper business, she chose the latter. The rest was, literally, history.

My mother is no Katharine Graham. The advantages she started with are Lilliputian compared with Graham's, for one thing. For another, her beloved husband, while often ill, lived into his seventies and did not die by his own hand. My mother never inherited a company (my father's business was more or less defunct by the time she was widowed) and never held down an actual job. But I've been thinking of my mother a lot—and talking to her a lot—while reading *Personal History*, because I had a sense (correct, as it turns out) that she thought of herself as a kind of Katharine Graham lite. Like Graham, she was the adored daughter of a hard-driving father; like Graham, she liked associating with the smart and powerful members of her world; although she was one hundred percent Jewish while Graham was only half Jewish, my mother had, like Graham, an ambivalent relationship with the religious part of her religion. One of the things I discovered in my near-daily phone calls with June this last week was that she had almost total recall for the book she read several years ago. (In recent years, an eye problem has forced this lifelong reader to rent and buy books on tape.) "You know that period when she was in Washington going to a lot of parties and dating Phil?" she asked me the other night. "That reminds me of the six months between college and when I married your father."

Never mind that the section that looms so large in my mother's legend is all of about twenty pages long and was, I bet, glossed over by most readers, including me. That's the great beauty of *Personal History:* because it is so long, and because Graham played so many parts in her life, there is something here for everyone. As far as my mother is concerned, the book is about Graham's childhood and her marriage and maybe a little about her fascination, apparently shared by all women of the time, with Adlai Stevenson. Meanwhile one of my journalist friends refers to the whole memoir as a "story of Watergate." Others see it as a kind of feminist anthem, proof that a woman can do anything she sets her mind to. No wonder *Personal History* has sold millions of copies and is cited as a model by every famous woman who sets out to write her memoirs. (I'm thinking of Queen Noor of Jordan and Senator Hillary Clinton, both of whose publishers have compared their memoirs to Graham's.) As Nora Ephron, once the wife of Graham's star reporter Carl Bernstein, said in *The New York Times Book Review:* "[She] had not two lives, but four, and the story of her journey from daughter to wife to widow to woman parallels to a surprising degree the history of women in this century." But a great life—or even two or four great lives—does not necessarily a great memoir make. First of all, it's not so easy to expose yourself the way Mrs. Graham does, to portray yourself, simultaneously, as both a product of history and a creator of it. It's even harder to write frankly about painful and controversial things and keep everybody admiring you in the process.

As I was finishing Mrs. Graham's very long but almost never draggy account, I got the idea that I would wait to write about it until I'd also read the newly released *A Big Life (in Advertising)*, Mary Wells Lawrence's memoir of being the first woman to own her own agency in the male-dominated advertising business. Lawrence, while half a generation younger than Graham, was the same kind of strong woman, I thought, and it might be interesting to see where their experiences and attitudes overlapped. And yet I only had to skim through Lawrence's book to see that the most significant thing the two had in common was—here we go again—a fascination and affection for Adlai Stevenson. (What was it about that guy?) While *A Big Life* is engaging, and Lawrence's world and accomplishments are very great, it doesn't begin to approach Graham's book in either readability or universality. It's not that Lawrence didn't live through difficult times; it's not that she didn't fight and beat odds; it's not even that as a journalist I have the uppity idea that the advertising world is inherently less noble than the world of newspapers. (Well, maybe I do, a little.) Mary Wells Lawrence, as a memoirist, simply lacks a couple of qualities that Graham has in spades: she's not nearly as reflective and she doesn't come close to being as honest about her insecurities and failures. Later, as I lined both books up here on my desk, I noticed something else: Graham's memoir is slugged "Memoir/Women's Studies," while Lawrence's is called "Autobiography/Business." A friend in publishing told me that these distinctions are functionally meaningless, that they're merely suggestions from marketing departments, and many stores ignore them when deciding in which part of the store to shelve and display books. But still, I found the categorization interesting for what it implied. *A Big Life* is one American woman's story. *Personal History* is the story of American women, my mom included.

The Clean Plate Book Club

I've been feeling pretty smug these last couple of weeks because I've done what I set out to do: to read books in real time and report on what I've read and why and what it means. And this week, I was all set to talk about James McBride's *Miracle at St. Anna*, the author's first novel, coming six years after his huge success with his wonderful memoir, *The Color of Water*.

I was planning to discuss "sophomore slump" and how a great reception for a first book can be a mixed blessing for a writer and his readers: said success is unlikely to be repeated the next time out. I so loved *The Color of Water* that I was sure I'd be writing that McBride was the exception to that rule.

Except that after a weekend of trying to slog through this novel about the 92nd Division, the only African-American regiment during WWII, I had to come to a painful conclusion: It's an amalgam of history, myth, and politics—and it just doesn't work. I kept trying, because I liked McBride so much. I didn't know him personally, but his memoir was so powerful and rich that I, along with 1.3 million other readers, felt as if I did. Saturday: an hour in bed telling myself that lots of great books start off slow (*The Corrections*, anyone?) and that I owed it to him to keep trying. So after a perfect winter lunch of soup and bread, I tried again. By page 60, I still hadn't latched on to any of the characters. By page 70, my mind wandered to the words of that song in *A Chorus Line:* "I feel nothing."

So I did something I have only in my maturity learned how to do: I stopped reading. Right there, on page 71, right after the hero, a brain-damaged soldier, encounters the little boy who will change his life. I might pick it up again, I told myself. And I might. But I doubt it.

Allowing yourself to stop reading a book—at page 25, 50, or even, less frequently, a few chapters from the end—is a rite of passage in a reader's life, the literary equivalent of a bar mitzvah or a communion, the moment at which you look at yourself and announce: Today I am an adult. I can make my own decisions.

In this, I was a late bloomer. As a reviewer through much of the 1990s, I was constantly asked if I finished every book I wrote about, and I could honestly say that I did. I felt very strongly that if I was going to devote precious magazine space to a book—particularly if I was going to say anything even a little bit negative—I needed to have read every word. If something was so unappealing to me that I couldn't get past, say, page 50, I'd suggest to my editor that he find another reviewer, the book was just not for me.

In real life, too, I felt obligated. Perhaps I'd paid upward of $20 for the book, or maybe it had been lent to me by someone I respected, or maybe it was the book of the moment, the topic of cocktail chatter all over town. Besides, I used to figure, someone has spent years and in some cases decades putting this prose on paper; the least I can do is give it a couple of hours. Maybe it was a girl thing, the same pleasing gene that makes me buy a weird asymmetrical sweater in an overpriced boutique just because the saleswoman went into the stockroom and brought me a couple of sizes.

Now, thanks to maturity, or psychotherapy, or the simple fact that as I get older I have a lot less time and even less patience, I have given up my membership in the book equivalent of the Clean Plate Club. If I don't like it, I stop reading. While I admit it's harder to throw in the towel on page 200 of the average 300-something-page book, say, than on page 50—"But I've made such an investment!"—I make myself do it. My only rule: I can't write a review of it, nor can I opine about it at a cocktail party, should it become a bestseller and/or the talk of the town. Even if, by that time, I have read all the reviews.

Letting myself off the hook has been beneficial in any number of ways, not the least of which is that it gives me more time to devote to the books I actually *do* like. And, I suppose, knowing I don't have to finish everything I start makes me braver in making out-of-the-mainstream choices in the first place. If I were still laboring under the assumption that an unfinished book would screw up my reading GPA, I might never have tried to fathom Václav Havel, for instance. (Never mind that that "tried" comes with an elliptical but understood "and failed.")

But I still feel bad about McBride. The only consolation I can offer him is that he's in very good company. There are lots of other "big" and "important" and "buzzed about" books I never got all the way through, books like Charles Frazier's much-lauded *Cold Mountain* (it left me, well, cold). Zadie Smith's *White Teeth* (interesting, but about three chapters from the end, I realized I didn't really care about the people). And Salman Rushdie's *The Satanic Verses* (I wasn't in sympathy with the Ayatollah; I just didn't get it).

And in every case, the sun came up the day after I bagged these books. There was no quiz in the morning, no Reading Police at my door. Not to mention that the books themselves went on to greatness and comfortable spots on the bestseller lists.

So maybe my abandonment speaks well for McBride. Odds are *Miracle at St. Anna* will be a hit, now that it is in paperback. And maybe I'll pick it up again. But I doubt it.

March 8

Hype

L ike every other business, publishing is susceptible to—no, make that dependent on—what they call buzz, the slow, humming interest that might someday grow to a dull roar and tip a book over into big-shot bestseller land. And like most people, even or especially those of us in the media business who should know better, I'm as susceptible to it as anyone.

So this week I read *Everything Is Illuminated* by Jonathan Safran Foer. This is the novel whose author was wet-kissed by *New York* magazine, the debut that got a front-page rave in the venerable *New York Times Book Review*, the book that as of this writing— a few months after publication—has sold an impressive 95,000 copies in hardcover and has been bought by a paperback publisher for just shy of $1 million. It's about a young American, conveniently also named Jonathan Safran Foer (get it? a shadow narrator), who travels to Eastern Europe to discover his heritage. His guide on this trip is a Ukrainian translator known as Alex, who provides comic relief along with topographical know-how; Alex writes in the kind of butchered Russo-English that will remind you of *Saturday Night Live*'s wild and crazy guys. He's sycophantic and hypercorrect and clearly sleeps with a (probably very old) thesaurus under his pillow. The two of them are the first post-millennial Odd Couple.

In a jacket blurb, Joyce Carol Oates said, "[Foer] will win your admiration and he will break your heart." The *Los Angeles Times* hailed the book as "powerful." Even the generally skeptical *Kirkus Reviews* called Foer's skill "extraordinary" and his debut "haunting." Amazon.com has picked up the buzz and packaged it with the very much better book-of-the-moment, *Atonement*, in a special-purchase deal.

Here's what my friend Rita said about it: "Shtetl, schmetl."

You know me well enough by now to presume I'm probably closer to Rita's camp than the *TBR*'s, and I am—but that doesn't mean I think the book's unworthy. I agree that it's impressive and unusual and very, very inventive. And while I'm generally opposed to obvious gimmicks—like a character who sounds like Steve Martin—I find myself liking Alex's sections best. Still, after the initial novelty wore off, I began suffering from eyes-glassing-over syndrome, especially in some of the old-country scenes. I was also underwhelmed by the denouement, billed as "a heart-stopping scene of extraordinary power." More than a few times as I slogged through this not-overlong novel, I started to sound like a Yiddishe grandmother straight out of Foer: What's with all the fancy tchotchkes? I like a story with a beginning, a middle, and an end.

So why is Foer the media darling of the moment? Well, let's

see, according to all the articles that have been written about him: he went to Princeton, and the book was represented and sold by a very charismatic New York agent called Nicole Aragi and, oh, yeah, Jonathan Safran Foer is all of twenty-five years old.

When I was twenty-five, I was toiling as an editorial assistant at a second-tier women's magazine, dreaming that someday I might get to write some trenchant captions about running shoes. So it's possible that a teeny tiny portion of my pique with Foer's success has to do with simple jealousy. I'm clearly not alone in this: just the other day, I was riding the elevator to my office at the magazine, and two youngish guys behind me were talking about the book: "God," said one, "have you read all this stuff about the twenty-five-year-old with the novel?" "Yeah," said the other one mournfully. "It can't really be any good, can it?" I listened in silence as they complained for fifteen floors and then finally I thought I'd try to put them out of their misery. "Forgive me for overhearing," I said, "but I've read it and didn't think it was the Second Coming." To which they responded as if I'd just handed them the Hope Diamond. "Oh, thanks!" the more dejected one said. "I feel much better now."

There's nothing wrong with being twenty-five years old and writing a book, of course—even if I, and, clearly, those guys in the elevator, didn't do it—and the world is full of people that age who found great success and continued to find more of it for many years afterward. Norman Mailer, for example, turned twenty-four as he wrote *The Naked and the Dead*, which many still consider the best of his many books. Philip Roth wasn't thirty when *Goodbye, Columbus* was published, and we all know what has happened to him. But there's something about the hype surrounding Foer—like that generated for another overrated book I already admitted to not finishing, *White Teeth*, by twenty-something wunderkind Zadie Smith—that reminds me of the old adage about the dancing bear. The point isn't that the bear is a great dancer. The point is that she dances at all.

But book publishers and their marketing departments need to seize on whatever they can to make noise for their books, and age (or its lack) is a good selling point. Look, for example, at the fanfare surrounding *Twelve*, the recent novel written by eighteen-year-old Nick McDonell. It was McDonell's age—even more than his extremely well-connected publishing family—that the publisher exploited in its publicity campaign. The book, about an Upper East Side Manhattan white kid not unlike McDonell himself, has reportedly sold 60,000 copies in its first months, been optioned for the movies, and made its young author at least twice as famous as more seasoned authors four times his age.

The idea, I guess, is to turn a book into a media event, but this is a strategy that has major backfire potential. For me—as, I believe, for a lot of readers—when a book gets overhyped, we get mad. We're a funny, cliquish group, we book people, and sometimes we resist liking—or even resist opening—the very thing everybody tells us we're supposed to like.

I remember visiting my mother in Key West a long time ago and running into one of her retiree friends at the pool. This woman was reading *The Firm*—in paperback, but still, that's how long ago this was!—and knowing I was a "book person," she began asking me what I thought of it. "I haven't read it," I said. She was shocked: "You haven't read *The Firm*? I would have thought some-body like you would have read this years ago!"

Never mind that legal thrillers are rarely in my must-read pile; the truth is, eventually, of course, I did read *The Firm*, in the same way that I eventually read Helen Fielding's *Bridget Jones's Diary:* which is to say well after the reviews had become birdcage lining and the store displays had been mulched. Likewise, if I hadn't read *The Corrections* before it became a bestseller and a cause célèbre, thanks to the Jonathan Franzen–Oprah Winfrey flap, I probably never would have gotten to it, so overwhelmed did I feel by all the publicity. Even more important, with a book that has been dis-cussed, reviewed, and parsed by everybody from Adam on down, you lose more than just your ability to shut off the noise and come to your own conclusions. You also forfeit the joy of discovery.

As a reader, I am always looking to be surprised, to be wowed, to fall in love as I did with *Whitegirl*. But if the first three rules of reading are location, location, location, the second three are surely timing, timing, timing. If you're reading way before, or way after (and I mean years after, in some cases), the hype, you've got a bet-ter chance to find satisfaction. That was what I liked best about be-ing a reviewer: because I got books in the galley stage or even, sometimes, the manuscript stage, I came with few preconceived notions. A lot of times, I never even saw a cover. So when, a few years ago, I picked up a plain red proof of a novel called *Child Out of Alcatraz*, because it was a provocative title, I was thrilled by more than author Tara Ison's charming story of a girl with a prison guard for a father, a girl who grew up in the "shadow of the rock."

I was excited that I had somehow picked it out from across a crowded room.

That said, hype surely has its place, even if all it does is make you skeptical. (Would any of us even know to create a backlash against *Everything Is Illuminated*—and even, in some cases, to read it—if it hadn't been shoved down our throats?) I met Leo a scant fourteen years ago, but he arrived with plenty of pre-publicity. The older brother of one of my dear college friends, Leo was known to a group of us as "the coolest man in the world," because of his work, even then, with *Saturday Night Live*. We'd never met him, we weren't even sure what he did (I remember thinking he was a gaffer or something), but we were impressed.

Cut to: Ten years after graduation. I'm meeting a group of old friends in a bar. My friend Jim arrives—with another man in tow. "This is my brother Leo," Jim tells me. I spin around on my stool. "*You're* the coolest man in the world?" I say, the sarcasm leavened, I hope, with a bit of brash charm. "You don't look that cool to me."

Now, I never would have even thought to say this if Leo hadn't been just a tad overhyped all these years. But it was precisely because of all Jim's advance work that I was intrigued: What, I wanted to know, is all the fuss about?

It didn't take long to understand what all the fuss was about when it comes to *Everything Is Illuminated*. As for Leo . . . well, the process is a little more complicated and is taking far longer. It's called "marriage."

Eating Crow

There comes a moment of truth in every new friendship, a moment after the initial bonding and sharing of life experience, hopes, and fears, a moment when one or the other friend does something that could threaten the fragile bond that has been put in place between two imperfect but well-meaning souls.

I had one of those moments this week.

My new office friend, Mary, gave me a book.

Looking back over the three months since Mary and I met, I see that this moment was inevitable. A temporary employee, Mary had come to the magazine to fill in for another staffer out on maternity leave. Because we had known of each other for years, and because we had many acquaintances in common, we initially sought each other out. It wasn't long before we were showing up in each other's cubicles every morning, stepping out for lunch or coffee in the afternoon, and stopping in for conversations about our kids, about the job, about stuff in general, throughout the day. Mary knew I was working on my book-a-week project—at this point, even the guy in the deli where I buy my breakfast every morning knew about it—and we'd often talk about what I'd read the previous week, or what I was thinking about writing. Mary was always interested and excited: "I can't wait to read it!" she'd say. "It sounds so great."

Then, about a week before she was due to leave, Mary reached into her tote bag and somewhat nervously, it seemed to me, handed me a novel by the name of *Crow Lake*. "I think it might be good," she said. "Anyway, I enjoyed it."

I guess I should take it as a compliment that Mary had enough faith in me, and in our friendship—not to mention in herself—to take the risk she did. As I was accepting the book that day, my mind wandered back to a story she'd told me a couple of weeks earlier, about a woman we both knew and didn't particularly like. (As I said, we were bonding, and there's no quicker way for two women to do that than to commiserate about a third.) In fact, Mary said, she had liked this woman—who we'll call, let's see, Madame X—or at least had thought there was a possibility that she would like her should their relationship continue. But then Madame came into the office all aflutter one day and said that Mary simply must, *must*, read this new book that was the best thing she'd ever read. The book: *The Bridges of Madison County*. "This was before the novel was well known," Mary explained. (And obviously, long before the movie, which even Mary admits was far more tolerable than the Robert James Waller book.) "I didn't know what I was getting into, so I went home and started reading. By nine that night, I had thrown the book across the room I hated it so much. And by morning, I'd become incapable of even looking X in the eye. How could somebody I like have liked that book?" Needless to say, their friendship sputtered out faster than the plot of a Luanne Rice novel.

My guess is that Mary had thought long and hard about giving me *Crow Lake.* Clearly she knew that between book lovers, a novel is not a novel is not a novel. It's a symbol, an offering—and sometimes a test.

I used to work with a guy who regularly stopped by my desk for reading recommendations, and so I devised a quick checklist of questions: Fiction or nonfiction? Historical or contemporary? Male or female? Once I locked in on his general criteria, I could usually choose for him (Nick Hornby's *About a Boy* was a bull's-eye; so, amazingly, was James Kaplan's *Two Guys from Verona*), probably precisely because I didn't know much more about him than his answers to those questions and I didn't have much at stake. We weren't friends, really, and the worst that could happen was our tastes would diverge, he'd stop asking me, and both of us would get more work done.

When real friendship is involved, though, the stakes get higher and the game gets harder. My friend Jessie, for example, has long been my reading twin. She always likes what I like and hates what I hate. When I put her onto *How Boys See Girls*, for example, she fell into a rapture over the book, became its author's disciple, and gave copies out as Christmas gifts. Ditto, because Jessie spoke so highly of an oddball novel, Oswald Wynd's *The Ginger Tree*, I waded through a slow opening until I, too, came to love the mid-twentieth-century novel about a white woman, a *gaijin*, living in Japan.

But with a history of success like that, the failures are catastrophic. "Don't read the new Anita Shreve," I told Jessie last year, but she did—and she loved it. Which made me question her judgment and then my own. Worse, she lent me her prized collection of novels by British octogenarian Mary Wesley, who recently enjoyed a brief vogue (in *Vogue* magazine, in fact). They were too Queen Mum for me, the kind of genial comedies of manners that are the book equivalent of a floral tea dress and a broad-brimmed hat. I couldn't get past the first chapter in any of them. Was that my problem or Jessie's? Can you declare a book accident no-fault?

An occasional disagreement over a book's merit should not be a big deal to normal people, but the people I love—and the person I am—are not normal: we're book people. To us, disagreeing about something we read is as shocking and disruptive as, say, deciding that we hate each other's husbands. (Jessie only half-jokes that when she and her husband disagree passionately about a book, she contemplates divorce.) I should let it go, or reconsider my feelings about the book in question. But I end up reconsidering the friendship instead.

Luckily, the situation with Mary Lawson's *Crow Lake* did not become so dire, though I admit I had a second surge of anxiety when I mentioned to another book friend, Laurie, that Mary had passed it along to me. "Oh! It's so bad," she blurted. Uh-oh, I thought, friendships at risk everywhere I look.

Crow Lake is a quiet, contemplative first novel about Kate, a girl raised by her two older brothers in rural Canada after their parents are killed in a car accident. Kate is now a twenty-seven-year-old professor of zoology, more at ease with sea life than with real life; on a trip back to Crow Lake, she and her much more cosmopolitan boyfriend are forced to confront the secrets of the family she's been trying so hard to leave behind. Like a lot of first novels, it's a bit overwritten and, like so many recent books, way too full of easy psychobabble. "I did not analyze my feelings too deeply," Kate says about her budding relationship, ". . . maybe because I was afraid that if I found I loved and needed him too much, he would be bound to disappear. People I love and need have a habit of disappearing from my life." Still, the story of the Morrison family, and particularly the portrait of the older brother Kate so loves, is compelling. By the time I'd finished, I'd written "Oy!" beside a dozen passages like the one above, but I'd also avidly turned pages, in a happily desperate desire to decipher the family's secrets.

I have yet to see any reviews of the novel, and I suspect that it will be ignored, or even trashed.[2] But I don't care that it wasn't good in a line-by-line way or even that the story overshoots universal and lands pretty close to cliché. I enjoyed *Crow Lake* the way one enjoys any dramatic tale about a complicated family and their complicated—though ultimately, basic—problems finding connection and love.

But the real reason I liked it was that Mary had given it to me, not so much as a literary recommendation as a personal clue. Like the Morrisons, Mary's family comes from a rural area—one in

---

[2]Then again, what do I know? I just heard that *Crow Lake* was chosen for the *Today* show book club. But here's one reason I love Mary: she didn't call me up to gloat.

South Dakota—and like Kate, Mary is fascinated by science and the natural world. (She's a hard-core, or as she would say, "nerdy," science writer by trade.) And while I don't know the specifics of her family life, I do know that she is at the moment caught up with her siblings in dealing with a dying parent. What had appealed to Mary, I now suspect, was not *Crow Lake*'s qualities as a piece of writing so much as its situational resonance to her own life. Mary was taken with *Crow Lake* because it reminded her in some ways of herself.

Mary no longer works with me and we haven't been in touch in several weeks, but because I've read *Crow Lake*, I feel like the bond between us is even greater. By giving it to me, she was telling me she trusted me to know her a little bit better, as a person whose interests and background were well illustrated within it. She wasn't making a literary judgment when she handed me the book that day, she was making an open gesture of friendship. So, phew: I can agree with Laurie, more or less, that *Crow Lake* is not a great piece of literature and retain that relationship, and I can go on liking and respecting my new pal, Mary. After all, what she'd said to me that day wasn't, "This is the greatest book I ever read." She'd said, and I italicize: "I *enjoyed* this. And I *think* it *might* be good."

Sharing Books Gives Me Heartburn

ary left the magazine before I finished *Crow Lake*,
so one of the biggest topics in BookLand was at
least temporarily tabled. When someone hands you
a book, is it a gift or a loan? That is the question. Is it nobler to assume the latter and live by the principle that all books are to be returned, or is it tacky and ungrateful to give them back? No one I
know would consciously borrow a book from a library and never
return it (even though you can buy a lot of old library books at
used-book stores and on Alibris.com). But a lot of those same
people think borrowing is different with friends. There's no return
date. No computer system. No librarian. No fines.

I believe that an unreturned book between friends is like a debt
unpaid. It can linger, fester, throb like a sore wound. The best pre-
ventive medicine is the simplest: Return All Books.

That shouldn't be so hard, except that the circumstances and
side issues involved in lending and borrowing are fuzzy. What do

you do, for example, if someone lends you a title in January but you haven't gotten to it by, say, June? Is there a statute of limitations? Do you need to check in with the owner again and see if you can get an extension on the loan? Will they even remember the book? Or the loan? Or that it was you who borrowed it?

It's complicated. Book sharing demands a level of clarity in communication that is often lacking in interpersonal relationships. I personally try to avoid these problems by not lending to or borrowing from people I don't know well and by reading what I've borrowed right away. This doesn't always work, of course, as evidenced by the "borrowed stack" I keep next to my bed. (Keeping nonowned books separate from owned ones is a recent rule, one that I instituted after I discovered a frightening number of volumes on the cherry shelves with other people's names written in them.) And when in doubt, I return. So what if Jessie thinks I'm an imbecile for muttering something incoherent about Ivan Klíma's *Love and Garbage*, which I borrowed six months ago and never read. At least I gave it back.

That said, there was a time in the early eighties when my friends and I were so broke that we had no choice but to learn to share. The object of our mutual affection was Nora Ephron's *Heartburn*, which vies with Fay Weldon's *The Life and Loves of a She-Devil* as the great revenge novel of all time. In any case, this was Topic A among my group of friends at the time. We all wanted to read about Nora Ephron because we all wanted to *be* Nora Ephron.

With such fond memories, I set out this week to find my copy of the novel, which was published in 1983. I face the mammoth cherry shelves, expecting instant retrieval of *Heartburn*. But for some reason I can't divine its location. Eventually, I do spot it, high up toward the ceiling. I pull the armchair over and climb up on its right arm. (If I were the kind of person who wrote "notes to self," this one would read, "Ask Leo to build library steps.") I pull down the hardcover ("First edition, acceptable condition, light edge rubbing, slight dj discoloration, light dj chipping," in the patois of used-book dealers). I think I even detect my friend Janet's scribblings on the back.

I open it and spend the morning enthralled.

Heartburn is great because nearly twenty years after publication, it is still achingly funny in a way that some later revenge-novel efforts have not been. Maybe that's because it is based very closely on events in Ephron's life. For the uninitiated: In the late seventies, two famous journalists met and married. The woman, Nora Ephron, had written many witty essays for *Esquire*, some of which were collected in the delightful *Scribble, Scribble* and *Crazy Salad*. The man was Carl Bernstein. Bernstein is, of course, half of the team of reporters who gave us "Deep Throat," made Watergate a household word, and brought down the Nixon administration. A little while later, Ephron and Bernstein had a son. Soon thereafter Ephron was pregnant again, and Bernstein began an affair with a diplomat's wife. Finally, Ephron left him. That's the story of *Heartburn*.

But what would have been a familiar sad story of the heart was given new life on the page by Ephron's wit ("The man is capable of having sex with a Venetian blind," she said of her philandering mate) and by her rage. This is easier said than done. Would that some later spurned-woman memoirists had more of either. Consider Catherine Texier's 1998 *Breakup*, for example, a chronicle of an extramarital affair and its predictable aftermath that was plenty angry, all right, but succeeded only in making readers cringe at the behavior of both the wronging husband and the wronged wife. Or Kathryn Harrison's *The Kiss* (and before that, the novel version, *Thicker Than Water*), in which the author confides details of her consensual affair with her own father. Even a Harrison fan—which I am—would have to admit that this book overflowed with a self-consciousness and affectation that couldn't cohabit the same hard covers as humor and pain. Like Ephron before her, Harrison was excoriated for writing such a personal story because she had young children, who might (might?) not want to learn, or to have their elementary school classmates remind them, that their mother slept with their grandfather. It seems to me that an almost equally serious crime was to write in prose so turgid its only purpose was to make the airing of dirty laundry look artful.

Ephron doesn't bother with artful. She just unloads the laundry—and it's as deliciously dirty now as then. She changes some names and probably leaves out at least as much as she puts in, but you would have had to be living in an Afghan cave not to know of whom she was talking—and to feel her pain. Back then, my friends and I—aspiring writers who had visions of being the Noras of the next generation—couldn't get enough. (Except for the recipes, which, like most people, we skipped.) The hardcover I pulled from my shelf today is beat up because it was passed around among us so many times.

If the definition of intelligence is the ability to hold two opposing thoughts in your head simultaneously, then Nora Ephron was the first woman in my adult life about whom I could successfully feel two opposing feelings. I admired Nora Ephron and I envied her. She was, after all, making it in the big time, which to me meant any world outside of women's service magazines and the style sections of newspapers. She was already a star, and this was before she became the top female film director of her time. (Sorry, Penny Marshall.) But her subject matter—life, relationships, social politics—wasn't intimidating. She was one of the very few female contributors to *Esquire* at the time, and the fact that she addressed mundane issues in publications that were almost exclusively male-dominated made her all the more enviable. We could do this, we thought. We're as funny and as smart and as engaging as she is.

Except, of course, that the kind of writing Ephron does in *Heartburn* and did in her columns is a lot harder than it looks. Whether writing about life issues big (her ambitions) or small (her breasts), she has an edge, a knowingness that we tried hard to emulate. In *Heartburn*, she took the ultimate chance: exposing herself as a naïf, a wronged woman, a loser. She remained winning. But it wasn't lost on us that a woman we so admired, a woman we believed to be so highly evolved and self-possessed, suffered the most prosaic of humiliations—sexual betrayal by a husband. A husband even more famous than she! (A husband being the one thing none of us had.) If this was the first time I showed signs of mature intelligence, it was also the moment at which I learned about schadenfreude.

My group of friends—Joanne, Janet, Marcy, and I—would dissect *Heartburn* the way little kids today discuss Pokémon.

We'd talk about the characters as if we knew them. We'd refer to Ephron's Rachel by her first name, as if she were in the room. We'd quote relevant passages when appropriate. "Why do you feel you have to turn everything into a story?" Rachel's shrink asks her about her wisecracking take on the disastrous marriage. "Because if I tell the story, I can make you laugh, and I would rather have you laugh at me than feel sorry for me," was the Ephronesque reply we would repeat every time one of us dramatized a minor incident. Passages like "It's kreplach, remember?" became shorthand for loosely translated Yiddish wisdom meaning, "It's still the same old thing, no matter how you slice it." *Heartburn* provided us with the mantras to survive young adulthood.

In fact, rereading *Heartburn* this morning reopened my mental diary on a five-year period I had thought I had forgotten. An old book can do that for you. It can help you re-create your life's calendar. (It's engraved in my mind, for example, that Philip Roth published *Patrimony* in 1991, because I can see myself lying on my living room couch on one winter day reading a galley and thinking how much I wished I could give it to my father, who had died just the year before and was constantly on my mind.) An old book can remind you of where and who you were then. It can define a moment in your life, as surely as the moment Rachel's marriage ended was defined by her opening a songbook to find an inscription from her husband's lover.

Sharing *Heartburn* is notable because it was so effortless and because I trusted the people I lent my copy to. I knew that Joanne, Janet, and Marcy were book people, like me, and that they'd sooner run off with Ephron's husband than with her book.

But I learned, the hard way, that not everybody is so highly principled.

As I finished *Heartburn*, I had one more mental picture: that of a twenty-something woman lending her only copy of a beloved novel to a man she thought at the time might be "the one." It turned out that he wasn't, a fact she discovered soon after she gave him the book. (Was there a connection?) He had told her he would return it the next time they saw each other. Except there never was a next time.

Months went by, and the young woman grew angrier and angrier. She began to leave messages on his answering machine. "I want my book back! Where's my *Heartburn*?" No answer.

A decade passed. One night she saw this man in a restaurant. He stopped by to say hello, bygones being bygones and all. "I look at you and I think of *Heartburn*," she told him. His face went blank. "You know, my book. The Nora Ephron thing I lent you. I'd still like it back." He slunk away, proving his own superior intellect by entertaining two thoughts simultaneously: (1) Who knows where the damn thing is? And (2) Was she always this crazy?

But he must have gone home and found it, because the next day an envelope containing the same battered copy arrived on her doorstep.

To me, this was a *Heartburn* moment. It had shame, betrayal, revenge—and satisfaction. I like to think Nora Ephron would have been proud.

March 29

Nothing Happened³

I'm like an animal off its feed. I can't get into a novel to save my life. Biographies bore me. I've left so many open books, belly down, on the green bedroom rug that the whole place is starting to look like an aerial view of a town full of Swiss chalets. I'm out of sorts. I'm off my game. I'm irregular.

These are the things I tried to read this week and how far I got:

The Red Tent (20 pages)
Invisible Man (3 pages)
Ulysses (1 page, which, come to think of it, is as many as
anybody I know ever read)
The Wind-Up Bird Chronicle (10 pages)

---

³My affectionate title for a slow, dense, but still wonderful book by Joseph Heller, which he chose to call *Something Happened.*

The Emperor of Ocean Park (300 pages, but the book is twice
   that long and goes from fascinating to stultifying so
   quickly around page 250 that I am developing some personal animus toward its author, Stephen L. Carter)

For two months now, I've made lists and piles. I've canvassed
my friends for recommendations. I've thought back on the books I
always meant to read and I've dug up books I used to love as a
teenager. I've ordered hundreds of dollars' worth of hardcovers on
the Internet and begged free ones where I could get them. The
stacks next to my bed are growing even faster than Charley.

So now I'm like the woman with a closet full of clothes and
nothing to wear. (Actually, I'm not just like that woman, I *am* that
woman, but that's another story.)

Poor me. I have too many choices.

"Take a break," my friends say. "Lighten up." To which I reply
like the surly teenager I'm becoming: As if.

I'm a reader, I want to scream. That's what I *do*.

When things go right in my life, I read. When things go wrong,
I read more. Frustrated with work, bored with my marriage, annoyed at my kid or my friends, I escape into books. But now books
are my work, my marriage and my friends, so where am I supposed
to find comfort now?

I know, I know. You're not very sympathetic. Why would you
be? I'm living out your fantasy: I'm getting paid to read, I have (or
have access to) all the books in the world *and* I have the time to
read them. So what's the freakin' problem? as Charley asked me in
another context last week. (P.S. I sent him to his room for dis-

respecting his mother, and he promptly picked up a Thornberrys joke book and started to, yup, read.)

My friend Louisa knows. A rabid book devourer like me, she finally landed a job reviewing for one of the trades. "Perfect," she crowed the day she got the assignment. "I can get paid for doing what I love." Six months later I ask her how it's going. "Ugh," she snorts. "I'm overwhelmed. There's a world of difference between reading for pleasure and reading for dollars. I should probably just start having sex for money."

Here's something I've learned: Having limitless choices is as difficult as having none at all. Maybe more difficult. They say the key to good parenting is giving kids fewer options, not more; that too many possibilities beget anxiety, and anxiety begets anger and more bad choices. Suddenly, I see what they mean. When I'm in this off mood, the sight of those bedside piles makes me shake. There's simply no way the books there won't soon morph into dozens of new houses in my little Swiss town.

So like it or not, I make the only choice of which I'm now capable. I give up. I give myself the week off. And then I do what any self-respecting New York woman with too many books and too many clothes does when she's frustrated. I go shopping at my favorite boutique down the street. At least there I find the limits I crave, or my MasterCard finds them for me. I get out for about $200, which is a bargain considering how many years of college my previous shopping sprees have provided for the owner's kid.

Now, if I could only figure out how to send the bill to the authors and publishers who drove me there in the first place.

April 6
Book by Book

The retail therapy was a useful Band-Aid, but the real cure came to me a few days later, when I'd more or less accepted that I would never read again. I looked up at my bookshelf to see Anne Lamott's *Bird by Bird* sitting there quietly on a high shelf minding its own business.

Bird by Bird is without a doubt the single best self-help guide I've ever read. (Okay, maybe it's the only self-help guide I've ever read, or read all the way through, except for a couple of *Women Who Love Too Much*–type titles back when I was single.) It's great because it's funny and wise, and unlike what I gather about most of that genre, it's actually helpful. I first read it in a single day, just after it was published, back in 1994.

I remember the day perfectly: It was springtime, I had a column due at the magazine, an infant son suffering from intense separation anxiety every time I tried to sit down at the computer despite the presence of a wonderful, loving babysitter, and a husband who was spending an awful lot of time working on the other side of the country. My work was not going well, and so I was taking a break by stopping into a used-book store on my way to the gym. On the review-copy table, I came upon a smallish hardcover by an author of whom I'd only vaguely heard.

I thought at first that the book was about birds or birdwatching or some other such pensive yet outdoorsy thing I don't do; I'm not quite sure why I didn't just put it right back on the review-copy table. Lamott herself might say that my finding the book was kismet, that it was God delivering to me exactly the help I needed at exactly the moment that I needed it. But Lamott, I soon learned, is on more intimate terms with God than I am and has a better handle on His schedule. I'd call my discovery of *Bird by Bird* simple luck, or maybe a good cover and subtitle.

Anyway, I bought it, started it on the StairMaster, and then raced home to spend the rest of the afternoon lying in bed reading and getting up periodically to run to the computer to see if Lamott had cajoled my muse into returning. She hadn't, but I almost didn't care. At least I was in the company of somebody who somehow, miraculously, seemed to know exactly what I was feeling every time I sat down to write: "delusions, hypochondria, the grandiosity, the self-loathing, the inability to track one thought to completion . . . and especially paranoia."

When I pulled the book down this time, I was suffering more from reader's than writer's block, but what I was feeling last week wasn't much different from what I'd been feeling then: I was idling, I couldn't get into anything, I was lost. And while I didn't remember too much more about *Bird by Bird*, outside of the name and one particularly resonant chapter title, "Shitty First Drafts," I had a strong memory of its value. As I remembered it, *Bird by Bird* was a book about what it's like to be stuck, and how to get unstuck.

My memory, as it turns out, was pretty correct. Lamott's central point in *Bird by Bird*, expressed over and over in anecdotes of varying degrees of charm, essentially boils down to the kind of thing your mother told you in the ninth grade, the thing Woody Allen said and lottery ads continue to reinforce: Eighty percent of success is showing up—aka "You have to be in it to win it." In chapter after chapter, *Bird by Bird* discusses all the ways in which we try to avoid the task we have ahead of us, whether it's writing a restaurant review, cleaning the closet, or yes, reading a book. In chapter after chapter, Lamott delineates the complicated, crafty, and often hilarious ways we try to avoid tackling the task, the anxiety we feel as we realize the magnitude of said task, and the pain of just plain sitting there and doing it, and then doing it again, or more, until it's finished—and we can start the whole joyous and agonizing business all over again.

The book, in other words, is about process, not about results.

Obviously, to judge by the phenomenal success of *Bird by Bird* (hundreds of thousands of copies sold), there are a lot of people who needed to learn the lesson Lamott was teaching—and my guess is that only a small percentage of them were, or wanted to be, writers. The things Lamott talks about in *Bird by Bird* are applicable to just about any daunting task where creativity is required, which is to say, just about any daunting task. Her genius is that she'd found a way to break down the anxiety, and amplify it with humor and self-knowledge, and show how she'd struggled to conquer it. That she managed to do all this in the first place is laudable; that she did it without making us hate her is awesome.

One early Saturday morning a couple of weeks ago, Charley announced to me that he wanted to go immediately to the bookstore to buy the complete Captain Underpants oeuvre, a collection of six quasi-comic books by Dav Pilkey, who has made a fortune by recognizing that little boys can't get enough of the word "fart." It was the first time he'd ever spontaneously made a reading request, and if one of the online bookstores had had a one-hour delivery service, I would have jumped out of bed to log on. As it was, I hopped in the shower, threw on some clothes and practically pushed him into a taxi to the bookstore. When later, with *Captain Underpants and the Wrath of the Wicked Wedgie Woman* safely purchased, he asked—asked, mind you—if he could sit quietly by the cash register and read while I went about the important task of buying deodorant and toothpaste and shampoo for the family, I did what any ambitious, readaholic Jewish mother would do. I qvelled. This is a kid who gets the whole concept of reading for pleasure, I thought. He's actually enjoying himself with a book!

A couple of hours later, Leo came home from the studio. "Guess what I did today, Daddy?" Charley announced. "Mommy bought me five books today. I've read three of them already. That's 150 pages in five hours!"

So much for appreciating quality over quantity.

When I took on this project of reading a book a week, it sounded like pure pleasure: reading whatever you want whenever you want to is the closest thing I can think of to a fantasy fulfilled.

But suddenly I was in a different place, as Lamott would say. What had been a pleasure, an enjoyment, was now a project, and projects by definition have deadlines and goals. All last week, I was obsessed not with the process of reading and finding enjoyment in what I read but with the fact that I was falling behind on my schedule, that I was blowing my deadline. I was definitely suffering from what I call White Rabbit syndrome, after the character Alice meets in Wonderland: I was hurrying, rushing, so worried about being late for an appointment that I lost sight of why I'd made the appointment in the first place. And it took Anne Lamott to slow me down.

When I read *Bird by Bird* this time, I wasn't conscious of really reading it. I mean, I didn't sit down on Sunday night and choose it as my book-of-the-week, which is what I've been doing every Sunday night since beginning this project. I didn't set the usual schedule: (1) Read book-of-the-week Sunday through Wednesday after work on the bus and at night. (2) Write about it on Thursday and Friday. My process this time was far more desultory: I'd leaf through a chapter or two, wander around the apartment, read a little more, have a Diet Coke, read, do an errand, and on and on. But guess what? By the end of the day I'd finished the book and was fairly bursting with ideas about it. This time, I hadn't had an agenda, I'd had a journey.

Life is what happens when you're making other plans, John Lennon once wrote. Put another way: Any writer who's honest will tell you that she usually comes up with her best lines or her important transitional paragraph not when she's sitting in front of the computer, watching the clock, or using the word-count mechanism in her word-processing program, but when she's stepping into the shower, making dinner, or cleaning the cat litter. Getting lost in a book works the same way: try to force yourself to get engaged with something, and you surely won't. But take your time and have patience, and you'll slide almost unknowingly into the right thing. You'll accomplish your goal without even knowing it.

That's what *Bird by Bird* did for me this time, just as it did all those years ago. Remember I said I spent the whole day reading it instead of doing the assignment that was on its way to being overdue? Well, I didn't actually finish that column until the next day. But a funny thing happened as the sky darkened on that spring afternoon. I closed *Bird by Bird* and went to the computer and wrote a long, funny note to the author, thanking her for this wise and understanding book. I don't have a copy of that letter, and it surely wasn't the writing project I'd gotten up that morning planning to do, but I remember it fondly as one of the best pieces of writing I've ever done, before or since.

April 15

Even Greater Expectations

O n a rare Saturday night out together—rare because the designer at *Saturday Night Live* is almost never available on weekends—Leo and I decided to go see *A Beautiful Mind*. Leo was interested in it because it stars Russell Crowe and because it had gotten good reviews. I had a double motive: there's the Crowe-is-beautiful factor, of course, plus the movie is based on the Sylvia Nasar bestseller, which I had just started to read.

Then a funny thing happened on the line to the ticket booth. *A Beautiful Mind* was sold out. It only took a minute—and a minor argument over whether or not we could handle the violence of *Black Hawk Down*, another movie-made-from-a-book I hadn't yet read—and we settled on *The Royal Tenenbaums*. It didn't start for an hour and a half, and the dinner we grabbed at a nearby noodle house ate up only forty-five minutes.

To kill time, we stopped at the Virgin megastore that is conveniently located right next to the Union Square theater. Single-minded as usual, I immediately grabbed a DVD of X, yet another movie made from a book, but this one, *The Autobiography of Malcolm X*, I had actually—and recently—finished. As we waited in line, I began fidgeting with a pile of books on the counter. *Straight from the Fridge, Dad: A Dictionary of Hipster Slang* read the fifties-like script on the paperback cover that looked a lot like a pulp novel from that time.

"Buy this for me?" I asked. Leo handed it to the cashier.

"You're not going to read it at the movie?" he said in a tone that sounded more like an order than a question.

He was kidding. At least I think he was, since he wasn't with Charley and me the one time I tried to read in a theater. That was last fall when Charley had dragged me, for the third time, to see Harry Potter—another movie made from a book, of course—just as I was reaching the denouement of *The Bird Artist* (which has not yet, as far as I know, been made into a film). I'll admit I maneuvered us to a row under one of the dimmed lights, and sneaked in a few pages just as Harry got to Hogwarts. But no one, certainly not my enthralled seven-year-old, was any the wiser.

Even so, Leo takes my weirdness in stride. I surely would have divorced him by now—or maybe it would be the other way around—if he freaked out every time I woke up and turned on the bedside lamp to read for just fifteen minutes before I turned it off again, convinced I really would be able to fall off this time . . . until, fifteen minutes later, I turned it back on again.

But there are some behaviors, as Winston Churchill would have said, up with which Leo cannot put. Reading while walking down the street is one of them. ("You'll fall down one of those open cellar-door things!" he wails.) Another is reading at the dinner table, which, thanks to our insane schedules, is rarely a problem, since I usually eat with Charley around six and getting him to concentrate on his meal is a full-time job. And while I occasionally do try to read in cabs, a lifelong tendency toward carsickness, rather than anyone's plaintive requests, mostly prevents me from doing so. I've decided to consider myself lucky that Leo's not one of those people who disapproves of reading in front of the TV.

"Of course not!" I say, faking umbrage.

Actually, *Straight from the Fridge, Dad*, with its bite-sized entries, is exactly the kind of book you could read in the movies, but out of deference to Leo, and to *The Royal Tenenbaums*—which, you might remember, starts every scene with a shot of the chapter of the "book" on which the story pretends to be based—I didn't crack it. But I wasn't sorry when Leo suggested we head right home instead of stopping for a nightcap.

I'm sure *A Beautiful Mind* is an important biography and I'm sure I'll get to it. But that night, it was all about *Straight from the Fridge*. The book was published in late 2001 as a paperback original by Broadway, home to Gerry Howard, an editor known for his off-kilter baby-boomer sensibility; this is the guy responsible for Chuck Pahlaniuk's *Fight Club*, as well as the little-known but bleak and hilarious satire *The Subject Steve*, by Sam Lipsyte. *Straight from the Fridge* is not something anybody would read all the way through in one sitting, but the kind of book that will have everybody quoting from it. Who doesn't want to know that "to boil one's cabbage" means to have sex, even if proper usage cannot be determined since it's never completely clear which gender has a cabbage that can get boiled. (That it comes from several blues songs, sung in the twenties and thirties by Bessie Smith, suggests the vegetable is womanly.) Another of my personal favorites: "Harlem sunset," which means, apparently, "bloodletting" or "knife wounds." I've had the book for only a few days, but already I've begun quizzing my friends. What do you think "fresh fish special" means? I ask, delighted that nobody knows. Then I tell them, triumphantly: it's "a bad prison haircut given to recent arrivals."

At this rate, *Straight from the Fridge, Dad* could become the basis for my own personal revival of Trivial Pursuit.

To work as a true parlor game, however, *Fridge* should have been published more as a thesaurus than a dictionary. As it is, the 187 pages here list the hipster expressions alphabetically, along with their meanings. How much more useful it would be to have the listings go both ways, so that when, say, you were looking for a word that means supercool, you could just flip to the S pages and find "hip to the tip" and "sharp enough to shave."

But usefulness was surely the least of compiler Max Décharné's concerns. In his four-page introduction, the Berlin-based editor displays the same "deadpan cynicism" he says describes the hipster mentality. In prose that can sometimes be self-consciously anarchistic—he refers to the Third Reich as "Uncle Adolf and his playmates"—he credits books, movies, and music as his primary sources. Authors Raymond Chandler and Jim Thompson are particular favorites, it seems, as are blues singers and the whole genre of entertainment known as film noir.

In other words, I set out to see a movie based on a book and ended up with a book that got its inspiration from the movies.

But I probably would never have found it at all if I hadn't followed Leo into the music store that night. *Straight from the Fridge, Dad* isn't ever going to be on the front tables at Barnes & Noble (I went this week and checked). It's slugged "Language Arts," which I'm sure rates a shelf or two in the back of the bigger stores, but it's not an area I or anybody I know frequents regularly. The unexpected way I came upon it seems like kismet: my list is loaded with "serious" books, "good" books, "worthy" books, but it's this one that appeared to me. Like the longtime dieter who finally learns to stop counting calories and let her body tell her what foods it wants, I instinctively opened this *Fridge*.

Or maybe I'm just the object of smart marketing. According to the Book Industry Study Group consumer-research data on book purchasing, such retail establishments as the Virgin store fall into the "all other outlets" not encompassed by such categories as "large chainstore," "independent/small chain," and "food and drug" stores. And the numbers of books purchased there are tiny compared with, say, the numbers purchased at Borders, down the street. But for specific books, with specific audiences, there's the Virgin megastore, the clothing chain Anthropologie, and even Blockbuster (where Simon & Schuster last year adroitly marketed Sumner Redstone's autobiography, since Blockbuster, like S&S, is owned by Viacom, which is run by—you guessed it—Redstone). Whoever comes up

with these ideas is what Décharné tells us is a "wig tightener"—
someone very impressive. These are marketing geniuses who actually pay attention to who their readers are: in this case, shoppers
more likely to cruise record and video outlets than bookstores.

Reading snobs, of course, would call *Straight from the Fridge, Dad*
a "nonbook." By extension, its fans would be "nonreaders." Your
snooty neighbor isn't going to talk it up at cocktail parties, and it's
not going to be reviewed in *The New York Times Book Review* anytime soon. And yet, like those smart diet strategies, it understands
that even the most committed weight watcher occasionally needs
a bit of chocolate. *Straight from the Fridge* can satisfy in a way that
all the *John Adams*es, *Theodore Rex*es, and Naguib Mafouz novels
of the world cannot.

So what if it's not *A Beautiful Mind?* At least it's the work of an
amused—and amusing—one.

April 22

And the Oscar Goes to . . .

Okay, so I did finally both see and read *A Beautiful Mind*, and I have to say that while the movie was entertaining for what it was, it annoyed me no end that it was so bowdlerized: this is 2002, for God's sake; is it not possible that the general movie audience could handle some of the facts that Sylvia Nasar covers so beautifully in the book? I'm completely in sympathy with the protesters who lined up to complain about the absence of any reference to John Nash's bisexuality, and I'm shocked—shocked!—that his marital troubles, not to mention the fact that he has a whole other child by a woman not his wife, were so glossed over. But that's entertainment, I guess.

I'm no movie critic, but I know what I like. And ninety percent of the time what I like is the book on which a movie was based, a lot more than I like the movie itself. That said, when I came back months later and looked at what I'd written here, I realized there are some good adaptations out there; I'm thinking *About Schmidt*, which couldn't be more different from the Louis Begley novel but still works, and, I guess, Michael Cunningham's *The Hours*, though the Bloomsbury-manqués may come after me for admitting that I didn't think the book was all that great in the first place. And then of course there's *Adaptation*, one of the wackier movies made from an equally, if differently, wacky and charming book, Susan Orlean's *The Orchid Thief*. Generally, though, I prefer to draw my own pictures of the characters and situations I'm reading about; in the movie, you get the screenwriter's take on the author's take on the character. It's all one too many steps removed for me, like a fax of a fax.

Still, I'm glad I saw *A Beautiful Mind*. It made me think about some other book-to-movie adaptations I've seen over the years and the awards I would have given out, if—if only!—I ruled the world. Some examples:

GOOD MOVIE MADE FROM AN EVEN GREATER BOOK

Compromising Positions. Susan Sarandon and Raul Julia were impressive as the housewife and the detective trying to unravel the murder of a local dentist. But the 1978 novel by Susan Isaacs is even better at addressing the universal question: Who wouldn't want to kill the guy who mucks around in your mouth—and gets paid for it?

MOST HOLLYWOODIZED VERSION OF A SURPRISINGLY DARK BOOK

Breakfast at Tiffany's. The original narrator in Truman Capote's masterpiece of a novella was obviously gay. In the movies, he's a hyperheterosexual pretty-boy gigolo played by George Peppard? Makes for a better love story, I guess, but a lot of the depth gets lost in the process.

MOST CONVOLUTED MOVIE MADE FROM A CONVOLUTED BOOK

The English Patient. I loved both, but come on: did anybody understand the whole thing in either format?

WORST MOVIE MADE FROM A GOOD BOOK

A Civil Action. In Jonathan Harr's book, I could read page after page of information about toxic waste. The John Travolta movie was more like garbage.

MOST IMPROVED MOVIE OF A TERRIBLE BOOK

A tie: Robert James Waller's *The Bridges of Madison County* (Thank you, Meryl Streep) and Nicholas Evans's *The Horse Whisperer,* a long novel that very obviously falls apart in the middle. The author sold the film rights to Robert Redford on the basis of a partial manuscript and clearly ran out of good ideas immediately thereafter.

I guess that's why they say Hooray for Hollywood.

April 3o

Dear Mr. Robert Plunket:

Y ou don't know me, but I know you. In fact, I am your biggest fan.

I love your book *Love Junkie* and I'm writing to tell you that from what I've noticed about the publishing business, you and your book are poised to become the next great (re)discovery. It's my prediction that in a couple of years, at dinner parties and in bookstores and probably even on NPR, you are going to be one very hot writer—you might even get to appear on *Charlie Rose.* I know this because I've seen this happen with many of my favorite out-of-print authors whom nobody ever heard of until some bored magazine or newspaper editor or TV producer got the brilliant idea to rerelease and repromote their books. I mean: look what happened to Dawn Powell, who was pretty obscure until old Gore Vidal started running up and down the country praising her. Look at Paula Fox, who, I'll admit, has the added cachet of turning out to be Courtney Love's long-lost grandmother. (Do you, by any chance, have any famous or infamous relatives with tragically dead spouses?) I know you're next because you have all the right stuff: your book is irreverent and funny and, well, peculiar. It's not for everyone—it's too raw and vulgar and silly. And there's nothing like a book that's not for everyone to make everyone want to read it.

You're going to be a major star.

But I want you to know something: I was there first. I also read and loved *My Search for Warren Harding*, I'll have you know. And part of why I'm writing to you now is that I know I'm not going to be any too happy when the whole world "discovers" your work and acts like they've known about it all along. Don't you hate when that happens? To me, it's like finding out that the great guy you met on a boat trip through an obscure South American rain forest, a guy you thought you'd conjured up out of your own imagination and need, ups and marries your best friend and then her sister and then her aunt. Suddenly, your secret love turns out to belong to everybody. You feel robbed.

I loved *Love Junkie* the minute I read it, back in about 1992. I'm not even sure how I came to read it, to tell you the truth, but it must have been a gift from one of my publishing friends, because all I found when I went looking for it last week was a set of proofs. (You saw the proofs, right? They have a red cover with a pair of lipsticked lips on it, which always sort of reminded me of the Rolling Stones' *Sticky Fingers* record cover.) I hope this doesn't offend you, but I think I was also drawn to it because of your name, which, just in case no one has ever mentioned it, is kind of funny. It makes me think of Esther Blodgett, the doomed Garland/

Streisand character in *A Star Is Born*, and of that jam commercial. You know, with a name like that, he's *got* to be good.

But I digress. The point is that I loved your book at least as much for what it wasn't as for what it was: a book about gay life in the thick of the AIDS years that was only very tangentially about AIDS. That's a pretty hard thing to pull off, Mr. Plunket, but you did it, even if the very few reviews published at the time were kind of snarky and dismissive about it: I hope someone close to you kept the *Los Angeles Times* review out of your house so that you never had to know that the critic called it a "très lightweight *Madame Bovary*" that seemed to have been "tossed off by its author in a couple of rainy afternoons." (She tried to make up later by saying you were some kind of bizarre genius, but I wouldn't forgive her if I were you.)

You know what I think? That reviewer—and also the one in *The Washington Post* who dismissed the book as "a lark"—didn't really get it. Didn't they know that the early nineties weren't exactly "gay," to use the old-fashioned meaning, especially if you were gay, and that a lark was exactly what we needed just then? Didn't they understand that a story about a lonely housewife befriended by a group of gay men was a great screwed-up parody of *Candide?* Didn't they get that putting a stranger in a strange land was the perfect way to lampoon that land? I mean, other books about AIDS were important to read, and I read 'em all—Randy Shilts's *And the Band Played On;* Michael Cunningham's *A Home at the End of the World;* and just about everything by Paul Monette—but none of them was exactly a laugh riot. They were more like the meat and potatoes your mother made you eat before she'd let you have dessert. *Love Junkie* was like the profiteroles you get served in mediocre Italian restaurants: flaky and pretty sweet on the outside, but surprisingly solid at the center.

I sure as hell got it, I can tell you. I moved to New York City in the early eighties, and for some reason or other—some say it's my Liza Minnelli haircut, but I vote for my, shall we say, rather dramatic manner—I've always had a lot of gay friends. I'm not saying that I was as lonely and pathetic as Mimi, or as much of a snob, but I, too, have been on the grand tour of the Pines, on Fire Island, and have hung around with people who could burst into show tunes at a moment's notice. As a matter of fact, one of the most important people in my life up to that time was a guy named Artie Bressan. Maybe you knew him? He was an operatic singer and a director of porn films, sort of like the character Mimi hooks up with in *Love Junkie*, except that he was a lot nicer. He died in 1986. By 1992, I'd been a volunteer at an AIDS crisis center for about five years and had long since taken the advice Artie'd given me way back in 1985: I'd stopped counting my dead friends when I got to two dozen. You could say I was in desperate need of some comic relief—and you, dear Robert, became my knight in shining armor. You sent me *Love Junkie*.

To be completely honest, there are other books that I remember fondly from previous readings, but they don't always hold up under rereading. (If you want to know what they are, you'll have to read my book, which is coming out soon.) So I'm generally not much of a fan of the book revisit: I always figure books are like buses and there will always be another one. And life is short: why waste time on something you already know, when you can discover something exciting and new?

This is blasphemy, I understand. Most serious readers have a list of books they go back to when times get rough, or they get sad, or things are just plain boring. Last week, for example, my friend Mark told me he spent an otherwise lonely weekend at his lake house "rereading John O'Hara." My sister Liza regularly rereads Trollope. There was recently a whole book published—Wendy Lesser's *Nothing Remains the Same: Rereading and Remembering*— in which the author revisits books from her adolescence and intellectual youth.

That's all well and good for them, I guess, but it seems to me that rereading—or claiming to reread—is just another way for some people to trumpet their intellectual superiority. To wit: have you ever known someone to say they're "rereading" the oeuvre of, say, Jackie Collins? When I was in college, I may have been attracted to the guys with a slim volume of T. S. Eliot in their back pockets, but I wasn't unaware that a lot of them were phonies. I bet you'd have been like my friend who used to joke about all the English-major scholar types—the kind who wrote 200-page theses on such arcane topics as "The Notion of Time in the Poetry of Keats"—who wanted you to think their first time around with important authors took place when they were still in the cradle. For them, there were not nearly as many bragging rights in saying "I'm reading *Swann's Way*" as in saying they were "rereading" *Swann's Way*—in French.

But then last Wednesday morning I woke up with a throat so

full of knives that I called in sick to work, something I hadn't done since 1986 or so. I felt so bad even my husband took pity on me and offered to take the kid to school. By nine A.M., I was alone, which, as even poor lonely Mimi would have known, is a rare occurrence for a middle-aged wife and mother. I guess your Mimi would have spent the time planning her home redecoration or answering a few of her porn-star boyfriend's fan letters, but that's just not me. I'm more the good-student, keep-to-the-schedule type, so I figured I'd stay in bed and read. I definitely needed some chicken soup, of both the actual and spiritual kind. Luckily, there was Campbell's in the cupboard and *Love Junkie* on the shelf.

I'm happy to report that even on rereading ten years later, the book made me laugh out loud more than once. I have this habit of turning down corners of pages that contain something I like. Sometimes I'll write in a book, but I try to avoid it. It's so *messy*. And on that day I spent in bed with the sore throat, I turned down a lot of pages. I'd intended to quote from them for you, but there are just so many! And besides, many of them are of the long-set-up, you-had-to-be-there variety, and I don't want to waste your time. Suffice to say the book struck me as funny this time as last, and reading it while I was sick was comforting somehow. It was kind of like meeting up with an old boyfriend when you're feeling fat and ugly and unlovable and discovering that you're still attracted to each other. It's exciting and familiar at the same time, a pretty great combo.

Which, I guess, is the reason people reread in the first place: they like going into a book knowing what they're getting at the same time that they can discover a line or a character or an attitude they missed the first time around. They like, in a world full of bad feelings and surprises, to know that the book they're reading will offer up none of the above. They like, in other words, returning to the known.

So I owe you one, Robert Plunket, first for making me laugh (again) and second for proving to my husband that there's a reason to keep all these old books around the house even years after everybody stops talking about them (if, that is, they ever talked about them at all). But you never reread, he says. Now I can look him in the eye and say haughtily, just as Mimi might, "Do too!"

May 5
P.S. I Lied

You know how I wrote that I'd read all those other books at the same time that I first read *Love Junkie?* Well, that's not a hundred percent true: I'd never actually opened my hardcover copy of Michael Cunningham's *A Home at the End of the World*, which has been sitting on my shelf since probably 1992. I'm usually not much of a liar; if you read my book, you'll see I cop to a whole lot of important books I've never finished, or in some cases, even started. But for years I just couldn't admit that I'd never gotten to *A Home at the End of the World:* I wanted to read it, I meant to read it, and I read so much about it at the time that I'd started to think I had read it. (This must be what the author Joseph Ellis meant when he tried to explain away his lying about serving time in Vietnam; he'd told students for so many years he had been in the trenches that he actually started to believe he had been.) Also, Cunningham's book was the kind of thing that would come up in conversation so often in those days, and so many people would nod reverently and say something about its being "one of the greatest books about gay life" they'd ever read that I found myself slowly over time nodding along with them. I mean, I never actually lied by commission, but I was happy to let people think I was one of them.

But I couldn't live with my guilt any longer. So right after I wrote to you, I went and got myself a paperback copy of the book (the easier to transport to work and back—and hey, tell Michael Cunningham to count the extra income as my penance for perjury) and raced through it over the weekend. And you know what? The story of two best friends, one gay and one straight—and the woman they both loved—is one of the greatest books about gay life I've ever read. I mean, it didn't make me laugh out loud, and I didn't turn back nearly as many page corners as I had in *Love Junkie*, but still I was very moved by it. In fact, when a friend asked me what she should read to help her deal with her son's recent announcement that he was gay, I recommended *Home*. It's just so rich with detail and character. I'm going to tell her about *Love Junkie*, too, I promise, but I think she might need a couple of years to get ready for that.

I hope this doesn't hurt your feelings. It doesn't change mine, about you or your work. As a matter of fact, I feel more indebted to you than ever and for more than "just" laughter. Because of you, Mr. Plunket, I've decided never ever to lie again about what books I've read. No more lies, I don't care whether they're of commission, omission, or schmomission. If I haven't read something everybody else says they did, I won't say I have. If I didn't like something everybody else says they did, I won't say I do. Nope. Not me. You're more than a great writer, I see that now: you're an inspiration. I mean, who'd have thunk it, Mr. Plunket? You've done something most writers never do: you've made an honest woman out of me.

Baseball, Part I

I'm sitting on a bench in a ball field on a beautiful spring afternoon when my cell phone rings: "Not now!" I growl into the phone to my friend Ira, whose name has popped up on the programmable thingy. "The bases are loaded, there are two outs, and it's *my* kid up at bat."

Charley—in full Devil Rays regalia, including the purple T-shirt he ordered me to baste up so that it doesn't hang to his knees like a dress—swings, in that tentative way that has become, in a few short weeks, characteristic. It's as if he doesn't expect to hit the ball and, ever self-conscious, makes the decision to stop midswing and shrug theatrically ("I don't really care!") to the crowd. "Strike one," the umpire calls out, and all I can think is I'm glad he's not the kind of announcer who apes TV sportscasters by extending the word "strike" to at least two syllables and relishing every one. These are the youngest teams in the Greenwich Village minor leagues, so, mercifully (I guess), they're still using adult pitchers, and the coach pitcher now throws another one. "Strike two," the umpire says softly.

Now I'm really a wreck. "Take your time, Charley," his wonderful coach, Jerry, calls out. I can barely watch, but since there's no sound of contact in the next couple of seconds, I don't even need to be able to hear. Charley has struck out. Again.

Or as he says tearfully as we head home a couple of minutes later, "I always strike out, Mom! Every time!"

I'm pretty shaky myself, but I try to pull it together. "All you need is a little practice, Charlino," I say. "Jerry is going to play just with you for a couple of minutes before the next game, give you some pointers." This is true: Jerry did say he'd "work with" him. What I don't tell Charley—and what he didn't hear, suggesting that there may, in fact, be a God—is the reaction of one of his teammates when number 11 struck out this last time. "Charley sucks," muttered the little brat. "Sucks, sucks, sucks."

Is there an adult alive who had a good experience in organized sports as a kid? Are there parents whose hearts don't clench as their offspring gets up at bat, runs for a ball, or reaches for a hoop, remembering in explicit detail the humiliations of their own youth? I suppose there are some—they're probably the parents of the kids who *never* strike out and who will, in my most dearly held dreams, grow up to be serial killers or WorldCom executives or both—but there don't seem to be many, at least not around these parts. Even Peter—Charley's best friend Luke's dad; tall, fit, rollerblading Peter—gets tears in his eyes when I tell him why Charley might be a little fragile in his postgame playdate that day. "Oh

God, I know," he says. "Every inning is like watching your life pass before you."

Nobody knows this better than I, who was routinely the last kid picked for the kickball, baseball, soccer, hockey, and whatever-else team. Chubby, self-conscious, and slow, that's how I'd describe my ten-year-old self, and I cringe at the thought that those words could apply to Charley today. I remember field days at my grade school with precise agony, and the memory of my brief attempt, in junior high, to be a cheerleader almost makes me weep. One of the "bigger" girls, as the coach politely called me to my face, I was assigned to the bottom row of the human pyramid that we were to form after a game; four girls would climb on us six, and then two on those four and then—the thinnest, prettiest, and fittest would climb up on top. The coach must have been hoping that my bigness meant strength, but he was wrong: Just as skinny, pretty Susie Q (not her real name) bounded to the top of the pile, my chubby twelve-year-old knees gave way and I slumped, bringing all the other girls tumbling down beside me. If the humiliation in front of myself and my friends weren't enough, get this: this was the practice at which they'd invited parents, so as I pitched forward onto the freshly mown field, the last face I saw was my mother's. And she wasn't smiling.

So maybe Leo's right that I'm projecting a lot of my own insecurities on Charley, but then, who, as a parent, doesn't do that to his kid? And besides, those tears welling up as we're walking home are real, and they're his. But I'm at a loss for what to do. My motto generally has always been "When the going gets tough, the tough get reading," but I've never been a fan of how-to books. Besides, I can hardly imagine poring over Baseball 101 at the dinner table. But then I remember one of the books I'd left on Leo's pillow a few months back. So after Charley goes to bed that night, I open *The Way Home* and begin to read. Who knew that a charming memoir by New York literary agent Henry Dunow would turn out be the perfect parenting guide for a mother in my situation?

Like me, Dunow didn't exactly come from a sports-oriented family. His father was a Yiddish scholar, a Holocaust refugee, who embraced many things American but never quite understood his young son's obsession with professional sports. In his household, as in both Leo's and mine, after-dinner activity just about never included the patriarch's taking his son outside to throw the ball around.

Dunow is very frank about having wanted to reverse this trend, and so he volunteered to coach his son's team, both as a means of bonding with the boy and of working out his own demons. The result: he was able to lay to rest some of his perceptions about his stunted development. (In a great aside, Dunow interviews other middle-aged men about their experiences. "There were no 'great times, loads of fun, swell camaraderie, character building, Coach was like a hero to me' reveries, he reports.") He was also able to give his son some of the closeness he'd so sorely lacked.

A friend of mine suggested that I tell Charley that it is the humiliations of childhood that a person, in later life, turns into art. I didn't see much point in trying that rationale on an eight-year-old. Nor is it useful to point out to said eight-year-old that he has many other, more important strengths, like an aptitude for math. ("I basically felt hated, like I smelled bad or something," one of Dunow's friends tells him about his childhood as a failed sportsman. "I was really good at spelling—but so what?") But that is, in effect, what Dunow did with *The Way Home;* he artfully deconstructs the myths of childhood sports at the same time that he shows you how to survive them. Whether he meant to or not, he wrote the ultimate advice book.

By the time I finished *The Way Home,* I found myself wanting to call up Henry Dunow and ask him to coach Charley's team. (I'd already realized that asking him to father my child whom he could then coach would probably create more problems than it would solve.) I settled, instead, for torturing Leo into, as Dunow's wife said, early in the book, "really being present" for his son. Obviously, Leo was not the type to sign himself up for coach the next year. (To be fair, he's sweating along with me at most of the games, but between his crammed evening and weekend schedule and his admittedly low patience level, he's not exactly coach material.) And surely, I'm not going to do it, even though my couple of outings with Charley have been beneficial to the kid in at least one respect: he now knows that there's somebody on this earth who's worse at baseball than he is. But if I wasn't going to turn Leo into Henry Dunow, I could at least prod him into taking Charley out to practice.

And so, one Saturday, the three of us trekked off to the sporting goods store to buy a brand-new aluminum bat and a handful of balls. (If it had been up to me, I might have borrowed some, or used any old thing, but maybe Leo was right: Charley wouldn't perceive the extravagance as pressure so much as he would delight in the specialness of the occasion.) Then the two of them went off to an empty field to practice and I went home to see if Dunow had any advice for nervous mothers. He doesn't, particularly; in fact, his wife, Wendy, seems pretty absent in this story.

An hour later, they were back. "I had five really great hits!" Charley crowed.

"That's great!" I said. "Ready for lunch?"

"Oh, we had lunch," he said. "We went for pizza."

Never mind that they'd been gone a total of an hour, which meant that they couldn't have spent more than thirty minutes on the field. The next day, as God is my witness, Charley got up to bat twice, and hit both times: a single and a good solid line drive to center field.

"I don't know what you did," I whispered to Leo. "But whatever it was, it really worked."

"You know what, Mom?" Charley said to me after the game in which he'd redeemed himself. "Dad showed me how to play better."

From his mouth, as they say in Yiddish, to Henry Dunow's ear.

Baseball, Part II

No doubt about it: baseball has become a huge subject in our house these days, what with the family's obsession with Little League and the fact that Hazel, our babysitter, is the kind of enormous Yankee fan that only a transplanted New Yorker can be. Still, if you'd told me, the least sports-oriented person in the world, that baseball would draw me to yet another book, I'd have looked at you the way Charley did when I explained that sleepaway camp was a place where you stayed in a cabin with a bunch of other boys and didn't come home to your parents for weeks at a time. "Why would somebody want to do that?" he said. The expression on his face, had he been a couple of years older, would have translated to "What are *you* smoking?"

But that's what happened: baseball drew me to another book. Sort of.

I was foraging for grub at the bookstore last week, having finished *The Way Home* and having that full-refrigerator-but-nothing-to-eat feeling, despite the bedside stack that never seems to get any smaller no matter what I read. At the top of a Quality Paperback row sat a book called *Facing the Wind*, by Julie Salamon.

This is not a book I would ordinarily ever read, despite the good reviews I remember it getting last year; despite my admiration for *The Devil's Candy*, one of Salamon's previous books, about the movie biz; despite the fact that Salamon lives in my neighborhood, patronizes the same hair salon I do, and is the mother of a little boy Charley plays with sometimes. It looks like a book about sailing. There's the title, for one thing, and the cover: a plain white front with a little postage-stamp-sized photo of a man and two kids next to a boat. Just in case you haven't surmised this by now, sailing ranks just above baseball—but a little below golf—on my snooze-o-meter.

But maybe because of all those despites above, I read the cover copy. Uh-oh, I thought: it's true crime, usually another skip. Why read that genre—or for that matter, watch reality TV—when there's plenty of real-life violence in front of you every day? Even worse, it's true crime of the most disturbing kind, the kind that involves inflicting pain or abuse on little children. (I had to walk out of the first movie Leo and I went to see together after Charley was born. It was Grisham's *The Client*. In the opening scene, a little boy is rendered mute—probably for years—by his witnessing of a brutal murder.) *Facing the Wind* is a book about a guy who cracks under the pressure of raising a handicapped child and one day picks up a baseball bat and kills his whole family.

It was the baseball bat that got me.

Maybe if Rowe had killed his by all accounts impressive wife and three children with a gun, or with a kitchen knife—or if the jacket copy hadn't mentioned the choice of murder weapon—I'd have passed on *Facing the Wind* that day. It was definitely the base-ball bat that impelled me to get out my $13.95. I hadn't thought much about this consciously—and I guess I blocked this out when thinking about *The Way Home*—but I've always been oddly aware of the weapon potential of sports paraphernalia. That must be be-cause I remember so clearly the time a kid down the street in my hometown got accidentally hit with a golf club and had to have a metal plate installed in his head; he lived, but the gossipy neigh-bors always blamed the accident for his under-par performance in school and later life. I'm compulsive about Charley and his new bat, too. I insist we keep the big bad thing next to our back door, and I've more than a hundred times chided him for swinging it around as we walk to the field. And just the other night when Leo was out of town and I heard a strange noise in the back of the apartment, I tiptoed out of bed and grabbed the bat to use as a weapon on the imagined intruder.

Maybe Julie Salamon, the mother, after all, of a Little League–aged kid, has the same kind of bat awareness, because she begins her meticulous recounting of the Rowe murders and their after-math with a history of that bat. Here's her first line: "In the summer of 1977, baseball was the only thing that mattered to Bobby Rowe and Jeffrey Mond [his neighborhood pal]." She then goes on to ex-plain how the two teenagers, in an act of friendship, exchanged bats (Mond's was larger and lighter) and how, a few months later, Jeffrey Mond watched from his window as police entered the Rowes' house and left with *his* bat in a plastic evidence bag.

In any case, it's a brilliant beginning to a brilliant and complicated book that is, of course, not about baseball at all, but about such enormous subjects as mental illness, the justice system, forgiveness, and renewal. The facts in the case are grisly, but straightforward enough: Bob Rowe, an attorney, and his wife, Mary, were raising their three children—one of whom, Christopher, was born visually and neurologically impaired—in a comfortable middleclass neighborhood in Brooklyn, New York. Successful and well liked, they were literally models of patience, good humor, and faith, particularly to a support group for parents of damaged children that Mary had joined. But Bob was suffering: in the fall of 1977, he began acting strange and hearing voices. He went to a therapist, who prescribed drugs, which he soon stopped taking. He killed his family later that winter, was sent to a mental hospital, and was released after three years. Eventually, he married a much younger woman who knew all about his past, and he had a child with her. He died of cancer in 1997.

So far, so typical true crime. But what makes *Facing the Wind* compelling is its psychological complexities: Does the mental health community deserve some blame for not understanding how dangerous Bob was and "allowing" him to live at home without his medication? Since he was technically found "not guilty" and released back into society, should he have been allowed to reclaim his law license and practice again? (Rowe lobbied hard, but ultimately unsuccessfully, for this right.) And most important, did he deserve to have another family and another life?

I got caught up in those questions, of course, and I was particularly riveted by the climactic scene in which the members of

Mary's old support group agree to meet with the new wife, Colleen, to try to "understand" how a good, religious woman could forgive a killer and trust him enough to marry him and have his child. But that baseball bat was never far from my mind: during the week I was reading by day, by night we'd watch the ball games on TV and read in the papers about the continuing feud between Mike Piazza and Roger Clemens over the throwing of a baseball bat. The magazines that week were also full of another innocent-implement-turned-weapon story: the case of Michael Skakel, finally convicted of murdering his teenage neighbor with a golf club. When Leo and I went to see Charley's final Little League game of the season—his team won, and he made two hits and one spectacular catch, by the way—I was unnaturally, even for me, focused on the aluminum bats the kids use. If the game had been a movie, the camera would have moved in on the bats and turned everything else into background, to make my point: These tools of play have a secret life. They can turn violent in the wrong hands.

I know this sounds slightly demented, but there's a larger message here: What draws a particular reader to a particular story can be completely idiosyncratic. (Note to publishers: Pile on the details in your jacket copy. You never know what will attract someone.) Reading is highly personal and often revealing. Readers have superstitious preferences and irrational dislikes. You can be drawn to a book because a character has your mother's name, for example, or because she has red hair like your beloved third-grade teacher. You can get turned off to a story because the hero looks like the last man who broke your heart. Readers, in other words, can be as superstitious as writers, or at least as superstitious as Julie Salamon admits she is. Nervous about meeting Colleen Rowe for the first time, she writes, "I noticed that we dressed almost identically, in the uniform of New York professional women: black pants suit. For some reason, this gave me hope." When I read that, I (a) liked Salamon for her humanness and honesty and (b) felt a little less ridiculous about my own.

Besides, I wasn't so alone in my bat fixation in the first place, to judge from the number of times Salamon writes about it. In addition to the opening scenes, there's a later heart-wrenching one at a showing of the movie *The Untouchables*, when Bob and Colleen watch De Niro, as Al Capone, use a bat to crack open the head of one of his hapless lieutenants. "That was life with Bob," Salamon writes. "Ordinariness mingled with horror." Fixating on the potential destructiveness of such an innocent household item can even be intuitive. When, after Bob's death, Colleen Rowe finally told her daughter about her father's first family, that they'd been beaten to death, the little girl had just one question: "Was it a bat or a hockey stick?" she asked.

June 1

Summer Reading

True or False:

In the summertime:

1. Public schools close.
2. Public pools open.
3. Many offices go into computer-sleep mode, granting employees half-workday or no-workday (or at least major dress-down) Fridays.
4. Families plan one, or if they're lucky, two, or if they're headed by very, very powerful executives, three or more weeks' worth of vacation.
5. Everybody has more time to read.

If you said "True" to all, you're in sync with most Americans. If you said "True" to all but 5, you're more like me.

Maybe because reading, for all its pleasures and delight, *is* my work, I find it harder, not easier, to do when the temperature rises. Summer's supposed to be a time you do all the things you never do all year, not a busman's holiday. And then, for me and maybe for others with small, only children, 1 plus 2 renders 5 obsolete. Yes, I have more time away from the office in the summer, but that time is taken up with more activities of the kiddy-adventure kind, like weekend visits to family friends and trips to amusement parks and other places where you're less likely to whip out a book and read.

You know how I know my summer has officially begun? Charley and I went away for a sleepover weekend at the beach with a group of his friends and their moms, and I didn't read a single word. Oh, I took a book, of course. Being me, I actually took two: Diane Johnson's biography of the writer Dashiell Hammett, a hardcover I'd found ages ago on the Web, and a yellowed old copy of Milan Kundera's *The Book of Laughter and Forgetting* that had been sitting quietly on the cherry shelves for years.

I'll spare you some of the details of how I made those two particular choices, but by now, you've probably gotten the picture. I ran around like a maniac. For a few minutes on Friday, Marilynne Robinson's *Housekeeping*—supposedly a feminist landmark—looked like the perfect thing to pull out of my beach bag in front of a group of smart, educated professional women. But I was also drawn by the one-big-book-and-one-book-only philosophy, which meant I should finally settle down with *The Brothers Karamazov*. But oh, there was also this new biography of Abigail Adams, which a few minutes of bookstore skimming suggested might break me of my aversion to reading history. But *Housekeeping* started off slowly, I no longer own my college edition of *The Brothers* (which

I somehow got a B.A. without ever reading), and the Adams biography was just too historical. Like the narrator of Geoff Dyer's hilarious *Out of Sheer Rage*—in which the author dithers for chapters about whether to pack the notes of his as-yet-unwritten novel or the research for an assigned biography of D. H. Lawrence—I shuttled around the apartment, putting one book, then another, into my bag and taking them out again. Leo said my insane scrambling reminded him most of my behavior at a Barneys designer shoe sale. "What the hell are you doing?" he asked. "You're only going for two days!"

"Yeah," I said, forgetting for a minute that I was about to join a group of three adults and four children who'd move *en masse* from living room to beach to restaurant and back again. "But two days of vacation: that's prime reading time."

While to me, they're oxymorons, the term "summer reading" and its close cousin "beach reading" are staples of magazine and newspaper articles from Memorial Day through Labor Day. Practically every publisher touts one "big summer book" in the hopes (often accomplished) of making big sales. The year Scott Turow's first blockbuster, *Presumed Innocent*, came out, I dutifully toted it to a long weekend with friends at Martha's Vineyard; by Saturday, I noticed almost a dozen strangers with book in hand, many of whom would wander by with opinions about who murdered the randy D.A. ("It's the judge," I told my host, knowingly, although I'd only gotten about halfway through. "Hmm," he said, clearly knowing it was, in fact, not. "How long did it take you to come up with that answer?") Never mind that the summer book of choice varies according to the socioeconomic, education, and literary level of the vacationers, there's usually at least one blockbuster, and it had better have page-turner qualities, which probably means it should be part thriller.

Some people, on the other hand, see the summer as the time to read all the things they were "supposed to" read weeks or months or even many dozens of semesters ago. Back in my Jackie Collins days, my mother would occasionally point out to me that Liza had spent her three months before tenth grade reading Proust. A couple I know who will be vacationing near us this August say they plan to spend their month reading, simultaneously, *War and Peace.* I've got big "classic" plans for our August vacation myself. But as Charley has taken to saying, "That will be then, Mom. This is now." And for now, I've got *Hammett* and Kundera.

I realize that neither of my choices meets the big-beach-book criteria—neither is current, particularly long, or as far as I can tell, about murder, a corrupt legal system, or adultery. And neither is sufficiently "classic" in the sense that they've both been written in this century. But they're both just out of it enough that their very obscurity seemed appealing. I liked the idea that my friends would think me unusual and sophisticated; I have a lot invested in people thinking I don't just run with the herd. And since the first question just about everybody asks me these days—at least as frequently as most urban professionals hear "What do you do?"—is "What are you reading?" I liked the thought of offering up titles these smart, educated professional women might know, but would most probably not have read.

Besides, while I wasn't riveted by the first chapters of the Hammett bio, I figured I might be able to use it to work up a discussion of well-known novelists' rare nonfiction adventures. (Diane John-son almost got a National Book Award for *Le Divorce*, which is one of my favorite fish-out-of-water novels, and while she has written four books of journalism, she's barely remembered for them.) And the Kundera: well, if it were half as darkly sexy as the author's *The Unbearable Lightness of Being* (an opinion I based on the Daniel Day-Lewis movie, not on the book, which I have never read), I thought I might get something out of it. That, and it's a very short book. My tote bag was already pretty heavy.

As it turned out, I should have devoted all this thoughtful en-ergy and corresponding bag space to something really useful, like an extra bottle of wine or the kind of toothpaste Charley will ac-tually use. Because for forty-eight hours, none of us smart, edu-cated professional women got through anything more complex than the newspaper—and even that was a sunscreen-blemished, sand-stained stretch. What we did instead was swim and bake and talk and drink and watch the kids jump waves and eat ice cream. Sure, I could have pulled out Hammett or Kundera around ten P.M., when we'd all retired to our respective beds—and I did think about it. But what would be the point? I hadn't brought those books because I particularly wanted to read them, I realized. They were more like upscale accessories, which, on Fire Island (as op-posed to, say, the heinous Hamptons), are about as important or appreciated as stiletto heels and diamonds at the beach. Besides, all any smart, educated professional women cared about by then was sleep.

June 22

A Million Little Pieces

T hings have not been good here.

Last night, Leo and I had a terrible Fight, the kind of Fight we don't have too often anymore, I won't tell you the details, but it started over something very minor and escalated fast. Words were used, by me and more loudly by him, the kind of words that Charley gets a quarter for every time we speak them, which thankfully doesn't include this time because he was already asleep.

After he screamed at me for a couple of minutes that of course seemed much longer, I went down to my office and I cried and I called a friend and I complained and I whined but because she is a good Friend and because she has heard all of this before, she didn't give me Advice, she just listened.

I was so keyed up and exhausted and mad and sad I didn't think I was going to be able to do anything but talk and cry but somehow after she and I hung up the phone I managed to pick up

the book I'd been reading which was *A Million Little Pieces*, about
a twenty-three-year-old guy who wakes up on a plane without any
idea how he got there. He has four missing teeth and a hole in his
cheek and he's pouring blood from every orifice and during every
bodily function and he doesn't know who put him there or where
he's going but it turns out he is going to a rehab center in Min-
nesota and his book is a stream-of-consciousness story of the time
he spent there and the struggle he goes through to first decide
whether he wants to get better and see his twenty-fourth birthday
or whether he would rather just let what he calls the Fury take
over him. The Fury is the little voice inside him, he says, that turns
into a roar and tells him to drink and smoke crack and turn violent.
The Fury has been with him all his life, but as he goes through rehab he insists on not being a victim and not buying into all that
twelve-step, addiction-is-a-disease bullshit and he insists to his
Parents who are nice upper-middle-class people who love him but
have never known how to deal with him and to the Counselors at
the Hospital that he is going to get straight without all of that traditional crap in other words on his own terms. And apparently he
manages it because at the end of this book when he tells you what
happened to all the people he met there including the young
crack-addicted whore he was in love with he also tells you that he
has not relapsed and it has been almost ten years. It is an amazing
Book that is written in this run-on style with weird Capitalizations
and Punctuation that is annoying at first but which you sort of forget about after a while but which I suddenly appreciate is hard to
pull off.

   I looked up and realized that I'd been reading for an hour and that I had actually been attentive to what I was reading and, more amazing still, that I was no longer sighing those big sighs I've always sighed for hours after any kind of crying jag. I was riveted by the author James Frey's story and I only occasionally got annoyed at him. He's awful and mean and disgusting and more screwed-up than anybody I have ever known but I think because he is so not victim-y and because his struggle is so real and palpable I found myself liking him and rooting for him. And I started to think about the fight Leo and I had and all the mean things he said to me and how frustrating it is to deal with somebody you love who has his demons and how even when he might be right about the specific things he's complaining about, the way he tells you about them makes what he says impossible to hear or deal with. And suddenly, this book which I'd liked plenty before last night was starting to make even more sense. It was starting to make me feel a little more sympathetic to myself and more important to my Husband, who has the same kind of Fury voice inside him. It doesn't tell him to smoke crack, thank God, but it's an angry voice and it makes him explode and stomp around and yell a lot and he has been struggling with his Fury for as long as I have known him. When I read Frey's descriptions of his Fury I know just what he means because I have seen Leo's Fury and seen him trying to battle it into submission and failing more than he succeeds, but trying again nonetheless. He calls his Fury "My Anger" and after it goes back to wherever it hides most of the time we talk about it as if it were the fourth person in our family, a creature who's away at college or something and only comes around every couple of months when it needs attention or money or to do its laundry. And I see him lose patience with himself a lot. And yes, I've seen myself lose patience with the endless cycle and the inevitable morning-after discussions and I have wanted to slap him across the face like Cher did to Nicolas Cage in *Moonstruck* and shout, "Snap out of it!" But last night, thanks to Frey, I was more tuned in to the incremental improvements we have made over the years, improvements that don't necessarily lessen how upset I get and how wrung out I feel for days after one of Anger's visits but do remind me that Anger is an ongoing struggle for him—and for us. And that if it's a struggle that is not ever going to be entirely winnable, it is a live thing and it grows and it changes and it's there and it's ours to deal with.

I couldn't stop reading *A Million Little Pieces* partly because it is a big, fat train wreck of a book and everybody, I think, gets some sort of perverse pleasure or solace, at least, from watching someone else's mess of a life, especially if it's worse than theirs. That's also the appeal of, say, Betsy Lerner's *Food and Loathing*, about her compulsive eating problem; it's also part of why I loved Caroline Knapp's *Drinking: A Love Story*, which has become all the more poignant to me since Knapp died, not of alcoholism but of lung cancer. It's also satisfying and hopeful to a person like me when, like Frey's, the wrecked life gets fixed—or because Frey doesn't tie everything up in neat little bundles, I should say partially and incrementally fixed. In a completely unsmarmy, un-Hollywood way (though, of course, a "major movie deal" for the book is in the works as I write), it is a positive and uplifting book. But the real value in *A Million Little Pieces* is that it explores and illustrates what it's like to struggle with a demon, any demon, whether it's drugs or anger or greed or food or something else that for some reason is a powerful force in your life. And that gives me pause. And patience.

At the very least, last night it gave me the nerve to turn out the light and go back upstairs, where, I had a pretty good idea, based on recent past experience, Leo would be sitting in the living room, spent by Anger. And we sat and we talked and by the time the sun came up we'd decided, yet again, to pick up the million little pieces of our marriage and try to put them back together, one piece and one day at a time.

July 6

The Time Machine

You can't eat pizza while reading *The House of Mirth*.

Some other things you can't do while reading Edith Wharton's classic about the beauteous, doomed Lily Bart: ride the subway, particularly if you need to look up every three minutes to check for your stop; sneak in a few pages between moves in a game of chess with your obsessive eight-year-old; try to open it anytime said eight-year-old (or even an eight-plus-something-year-old) is watching TV in your room.

You have to have long stretches of uninterrupted time to read *The House of Mirth*. You also have to have quiet. A long, rainy weekend afternoon would work. So would a couple of luxuriously sleepless nights in a well-appointed, comfortable bed.

I figured this out last week—okay, maybe it took me two weeks—when I set out to read the 1905 novel in my usual manner: here and there throughout the course of the day, during slow periods at the office, over Lean Cuisines long after Charley had gone to bed and Leo was safely ensconced at the NBC studio, while listening to the morning and/or late-night news. But I kept getting stalled: the phone would ring, or some pressing piece of business would seize my attention. It's not that I wasn't immediately riveted by Ms. Bart's plucky but ultimately sad descent into poverty and death as a victim of the sexist society. I was. It was just that Mrs. Wharton's book isn't meant to be read in fits and starts. She writes in long sentences, long paragraphs, and long chapters, and if you lose the thread, you sometimes have to go back several pages to remind yourself whose story you're hearing.

The House of Mirth was written in a time when reading was the entertainment of choice, when women like me didn't have bosses to placate and TV shows to keep up with and hungry kids wanting dinner. (Okay, maybe they had the kids, but they also, most of them, had servants to make them the dinner.) It was written by a rich woman about rich women for rich women who had nothing but the time on their hands to read it.

The House of Mirth did not, in other words, anticipate the reading habits of the multitasking, attention-span-deprived MTV generation.

Which is interesting, since I chose the book on the suggestion of a half-dozen people smack in the middle of that age group. It was, in fact, one of several books passionately recommended by Roxanne Coady, the owner of the R. J. Julia bookstore in Madison, Connecticut, at a special meeting in her store to talk about perfect book-club books. (Roxanne is one of the few people I know who, like me, uses books as her litmus test to judge new friends and acquaintances. Somebody else might check out a newcomer's hairstyle, or outfit, or taste in jewelry to determine whether she's bonding material; Roxanne and I became what I suspect will be lifelong friends when I mentioned, in passing, that Bernard Lefkowitz's *Our Guys* is one of my favorite books.) "It's a big old soap opera," added my friend Ruth. "Oh," said one woman I had lunch with a few days later—a thirty-something writer of a contemporary novel of manners not fit to wrap Wharton's masterpiece. "Have you got a treat in store for you!"

The House of Mirth is a treat—a long, detailed, funny, depressing, meaningful story about a hollow society and the way it ruins a beautiful young woman who is, to quote the scholar and professor R. W. B. Lewis, "admirable, touching, exasperating, forlorn, sturdy, woefully self-deceptive, imprudent, finely proud, intuitive . . . [which is to say] humanly adorable." Lily Bart is a twenty-nine-year-old orphaned beauty who lives with her punitive but reasonably well-off aunt in New York at the turn of the nineteenth century. She is a "smart" girl in the sense of the word that means witty and charming, a welcome "extra woman" at dinner parties and country weekends. Lily has no dearth of suitors, but she is particular. She knows that to improve her station—and, not incidentally, to pay off the debts she has incurred by keeping up all the appearances required of girls on the marriage circuit (lucky for Lily: she and the world were too young to know about Botox)—she must marry "well" (i.e., rich). But she is also vain and self-obsessed and almost knowingly naïve: she's too smart to get sexually involved with men, but she gets close enough to some dangerous ones so that she suffers the same fate she'd have suffered if she'd been promiscuous: she gets investment help from a man who tries to exact the usual sexual payment for his efforts. The victim of gossip and blackmail, a ruined and despondent Lily dies a horrible, lonely, and self-imposed death.

Everybody and her English teacher has by now weighed in on *The House of Mirth;* the Modern Library edition I read last week includes essays by the poet and critic Elizabeth Hardwick, as well as reviews of the book at the time it was published, and snippets of commentary by such lit luminaries as Professor Lewis. In fact, I'm starting to think I'm the only person over the age of twelve who has never read it: I've noticed that there are at least a dozen Web sites that discuss the book, my favorite being sparknotes.com. That's one of those sites at which people (they sound like high school students) send in questions like "Help! I have a paper due on this book; can anyone tell me its themes?" Or a more sophisticated version, also clearly from a young reader: "Would Thoreau like the world that Wharton depicts, one depenant [*sic*] on performance and image? Why or why not? This is really important. I need a thesis. I am stuck." Obviously, the book has long been required reading for everybody from precocious ninth-graders to prisoners on the college-equivalency track to professors seeking tenure.

I've never been in a book club, but I have seen them on TV. And I can understand why *The House of Mirth* is a very popular choice. It raises so many universal questions about subjects—like love and money—of interest to everybody. How much responsibility should Lily bear for her own demise? Is she a victim of her own avariciousness, or is she simply a naïf? I can just hear the forks coming to a screeching halt on the dessert plates when one book-club member offers up evidence that Lily Bart, in many ways, *c'est moi!* Everybody knows or has been someone as vain but self-aware as Lily. Who hasn't shared a meal or an apartment or an office with a single woman who, in Elizabeth Hardwick's words, has "been on the town too long"? Who has never experienced or encountered Lily's peculiar mixture of desperation and pickiness when it comes to love? We just talk differently today, that's all. Lily declares a suitor unsuitable because his bank account is too small; my friend Margaret rejects a guy because she once saw him in his apartment wearing yellow sweatpants. Wharton writes that "Lily understood that beauty is only the raw material of conquest, and that to convert it into success other arts are required." Here's a magazine-cover line I heard screaming from the newsstand the other day: "Beauty Is Not Enough!" it announced. "10 Ways to Work with It!"

So it doesn't surprise me that *The House of Mirth* remains, almost a century after its publication, the kind of book people still talk about and want to read, even if, unlike the students on sparknotes. com, they are not going to be tested on it later. There's the feminist element, of course—"Man, that woman got shafted!" was the single comment of an aggressively PC male friend of mine—and then there's the sheer joy of meeting a character who is a curious yet common combination of contradictory traits: self-knowing but naïve, ambitious yet at the same time pure of heart.

What does surprise me, though, is that for all its universality, *The House of Mirth* is not an easy or a quick read, and it requires a kind of concentration the common wisdom holds people won't apply to books anymore. And this, I realize, is also part of its appeal to book-clubbers, who, I'm told, sometimes need some deadlines and incentives to keep on reading. Even I, with whole days to turn pages and ruminate, had to make myself some rules for *The House of Mirth*, rules like setting the clock for five-thirty A.M. instead of six, so I could get in some quiet reading time before Charley got up. Rules like no more than one glass of wine at dinner so that I could concentrate on Wharton's stately prose without dozing off too early at night. Rules like absolutely *no distractions*, which means no peeking at other books, and absolutely *no double-booking*.

For a while, I'm proud to say, I stuck with the program pretty well. But then midway through my first Wharton week, a friend sent me a copy of the couldn't-be-more-different *How to Lose Friends and Alienate People*. It's a memoir by journalist Toby Young about his stint as an editor at *Vanity Fair*. (Hmm. A title stolen from another old book. Coincidence or kismet? You decide.) Cursing myself, I put Wharton aside for a bit of Young, vowing to read just a chapter or two before getting back to the Real Thing. There'd be no conflation problems, I was sure: Wharton was too good and Young too glib: they didn't even live in the same century.

"Toby Young's book is surprisingly sweet," I told a friend with whom I was lunching one day that week. "And he really understands our shallow, celebrity-obsessed culture." Then I went home and picked up my book and read a passage about "a world in which conspicuousness passed for distinction and the society column had become the role of fame." But for the different typeface,

I would have sworn I was reading a line from the oh-so-modern *How to Lose Friends*. But no: this wise observation was quietly buried in my homework assignment: it comes directly from *The House of Mirth*.

I'm just glad I stuck with the book long enough to find it.

July 20

Reading Confidential

For a few days last week, I wanted to be just like Anthony Bourdain. I don't mean that I wanted to cook in a famous Manhattan restaurant like Les Halles, where Bourdain is executive chef. Or to wear way too much jewelry for my age and gender, as Bourdain does, or to chain-smoke my way through life. (I've just given that up, in fact. But check back with me next week.) I was thinking I wanted to be like Bourdain when I grow up (never mind that we're within a couple of years of each other) in the sense that I want to have his energy, his irreverence, and his nerve. I want to write a book like *Kitchen Confidential*.

Kitchen Confidential, which lots of people read when it came out in hardcover in 2000 and/or when it was excerpted, several times, in *The New Yorker*, is Bourdain's memoir of becoming a chef; it chronicles what really goes on in the kitchens of restaurants that make you wait weeks to get reservations. It's an upscale tell-all with attitude, a *Fast Food Nation* on steroids.

I'd heard of the book, of course, but I hadn't read it, partly because almost immediately after publication it became something
of a phenomenon, and you know by now how I feel about publishing phenomena. Besides, I'm not much of a foodie, preferring
instead to think of myself as a typical contemporary American
woman, which is to say one who has a love/hate relationship with
food. You can't have grown up the way I did—the chubby daughter of an extremely weight-conscious mother—and be anything
else. Thanks to years of being told that sauces, sweets, and anything
else that tastes good should be off-limits—and seeing the proof of
same on my hips and thighs—my relationship with what I put in
my mouth is, at best, fraught with trauma. I remember, for example, reading an article years ago in *New York Woman* magazine in
which the author quoted a woman as saying her therapeutic goal
in life was to stop seeing a bowl of noodles as the enemy. "But it is
the enemy, isn't it?" I remember thinking.

Consequently, I don't read cookbooks, and when I inadvertently
stumble onto something about food or foodies, I have a weird take.
In *Stuffed*, for example, a charming memoir by Patricia Volk about
growing up in a family of restaurateurs, I found myself much less
interested in the anecdotes about the relative who was the first
person to bring whitefish to America than in the all-consuming
(to me) question "When your business is food, how do you keep
from getting fat?" Volk doesn't talk much about the food–fat connection, but the one anecdote I remember best, all these months
later, is about how she kept a precious piece of paper in a locked
box. Was the note about a favorite family recipe or some other
delightful heirloom? No, the paper had a number on it—143, I

think it was—which turned out to be the most she had ever weighed.

Needless to say, I don't cook either, although I do know that a number of women with my pathology do, probably on the theory that "those who can't eat can at least feed others." Cooking is Leo's department, and while I often do ask him questions about what he's making, they're usually the kind guaranteed to make him crazy. "You put butter on the vegetables?" I'll say. When he nods casually, I respond as if he'd said he'd put Charley to bed in the washing machine.

Still, my job requires me to eat out a lot, and when I do, it's usually in exactly the kind of restaurants Bourdain talks about in his book. In fact, as I read along, I realized I'm probably exactly the kind of diner Bourdain hates. I've been a sauce-on-the-sider and have, depending on the diet I'm on that week, ordered the "vegetarian plate." I often choose the plain fish entrée, no matter what the day of the week, and Bourdain says you should never order it on Monday, because it has probably been sitting around all weekend. Other things I often do that I'm not supposed to, says Bourdain: order meat well-done (the cook saves all the worst parts of the beef for this very occasion) and eat brunch *ever*. (Cooks throw any old scraps together for those "special" meals.)

So I'm clearly not Bourdain's ideal diner. Nor would I seem to be his ideal reader. But last week I was between books, as they say, and in desperate need of something to cleanse my palate after the rather hearty meal that was *The House of Mirth*. There in my local bookstore stood Bourdain—or at least his photographic equiva-

lent—decked out in chef's whites, holding the characteristic cigarette, and glaring at the camera. Now, that's my kind of guy, I
thought, even before I realized he was *that* guy, the hard-drinking,
tough-talking, chain-smoking chef who'd spilled the beans on the
restaurant biz and was now something of a national celebrity. To
me he looked a lot like a guy I'd dated in the eighties.

Hmmm. Maybe I didn't want to *be* Bourdain so much as I
wanted to be *with* him. For better or worse, I'd always been drawn
to men who had, as a friend of mine once said, "something mean
around the mouth."

I knew, going in, that Bourdain's attitude toward food was obviously going to be very different from mine, but I could also tell,
right off, that he had the kind of rough irreverence that's as delicious—and forbidden—as hollandaise sauce. Here's how *Kitchen
Confidential* starts: "My first indication that food was something
other than a substance one stuffed in one's face when hungry—
like filling up at a gas station—came after fourth grade in elementary school." Something about that "substance one stuffed in one's
face" and the allusion to a grubby gas station indicated that more
aggressively down-and-dirty revelations were to come. How could
I do anything but crawl into bed on that rainy afternoon and start
to read?

A few hours later, Charley came home from school and Leo
called from the office. What do you want to do about dinner? my
husband asked. "I don't care as long as we don't eat out," I told him.

I'm clearly not the only person enthralled with *Kitchen Confidential;* the book has sold hundreds of thousands of copies. And I'd

bet I'm not the only woman drawn to Bourdain himself, who portrays himself as the ultimate bad boy who delights in playing the cowboy. He's fearless: he names a lot of names (of restaurants, if not always of the people who owned or worked in them), and when he must resort to pseudonyms—I'd bet on his lawyer's, not his own, suggestion—he uses amusing, colorful ones like Big Foot and Adam Real-Last-Name-Unknown. He's funny when he tells stories that make his friends and himself look silly or bad—I'm thinking of the interview he had with the steak-house owner who Bourdain thought asked him, "What do you know about me?" when in fact, he was posing a much more innocent, and ultimately relevant, question. And he never, ever apologizes. Like every rough-hewn bad boy every well-bred woman ever loved, he comes off as an affectionate outlaw, a college-educated punk who is just a little tiny bit too cool for cooking school.

In her guide to writing *The Forest for the Trees*, the editor-turned-agent Betsy Lerner says that a memoirist fails the minute he or she compromises a single adjective in an effort to protect someone else's feelings. I don't know if somebody said that to Bourdain, or if he instinctively knew it, but it's clearly a dictum he lives by. I'm sure there are a lot of people whose feelings he hurt in *Kitchen Confidential*, and there are surely people turned off by his arrogance and vulgarity, but I'm equally sure his response would be, "Well, fuck 'em if they can't take a joke." His mission here was to tell the truth—his truth, maybe, but that counts. And the book works because he's a bona fide hyped-up, foulmouthed raconteur—and plenty proud of it.

In fact, if there's a flaw in *Kitchen Confidential*, it's that at times Bourdain seems too proud of his swashbuckling ways. I have to confess that I started to like him a little less as time went on and he drank, smoked, and caroused his way through another year. (And I couldn't help thinking how his long-suffering wife must have felt while he did it, and then when he told the world about it.) After a while, too, his tales of kitchen debauchery started to feel more truish than true. Did one of Bourdain's cook friends really lock eyes with a bride mid-reception and take her outside to go at it against a dumpster, while all his cronies looked on? I'd begun to have doubts.

In other words, after a while, Anthony Bourdain—or at least the persona he'd constructed in these pages—started to annoy me, in much the way that that old boyfriend ultimately did. He started to seem just a little too macho and a little too tough. He had a sharp answer or a quick judgment for everything and I wanted him to calm down and stop acting like the very poseurs he so gleefully exposes in the book. Like a woman who has finally had her fill of bad-guy cowboys, I wanted to be with someone gentle and calm and just a little bit more real.

So I guess I don't want to be with Anthony Bourdain after all, and I know I don't want to be like him. But I still appreciate his book, and not only because I now know to order plain chicken on Mondays. I appreciate *Kitchen Confidential* more because I found it instructive: it reminded me that most books—but memoirs in particular—are all about the voice, and that you can't worry what other people are going to think about you if you tell your version of the truth. His subject is food and mine is books, but the same principles apply: you have to treat your subject with fearlessness and attitude and energy. Whether your industry's sacred cows are beef or, say, novels that are just said to be "well-done," you have to skewer them.

Who knew a cook would teach me how to write?

Anna, Emma, and Me

One of the good things about having a partner who is just a tiny bit oblivious to the links between reading and life is that he doesn't take particular note that the two books you've brought on your three-week family vacation are *Anna Karenina* and *Madame Bovary*.

In my imagination—the one where my life is a sitcom—Leo would notice me piling the two classics about adultery on the bedside table in our new rented master bedroom on Fire Island and would turn into Paul Reiser or Will from *Will & Grace* or somebody and ask, "Hey, what's with the books about cheating? You tryin' to tell me something?" And I'd say, "No, of course not, honey," but then the twenty-seven-minute plot would reveal that, well, he didn't believe me and was in fact running around misreading all sorts of innocent remarks and behaviors and had worked himself into a good righteous frenzy before his folly was revealed in some meet-cute way. Then we'd make up and live happily ever after.

In case you (like me) somehow got through college without reading either novel, *Anna Karenina* is a long, most people think brilliant, nineteenth-century book about an upper-class Russian woman and mother who is married to a good though boring guy when she meets, on a train, the love of her life, the dashing Count Vronsky. Overpowered by a love she tries but fails to resist, she blows up her life and family to be with her beloved, only to become disillusioned and depressed and to throw herself under the wheels of another train. (Actually, the book is about a lot more than that, I discovered: it's about politics and custom and agriculture, and there are a number of subplots, but, let's face it, it's the romance that most people read it for.) For all its surface similarities—Emma Bovary is an unhappy wife who resorts to adultery and ends up like Anna, a suicide—Flaubert's classic is a little different: his Emma is not nobly tortured by her infidelities so much as not satisfied by them. She's a woman of appetites that can never be sated. She is, as I told my friend Louisa, like Bill Clinton in a nineteenth-century French dress.

One of my most dearly held beliefs is that anybody who's been married more than a couple of years who says she's never considered adultery is either (a) a saint or (b) a liar or (c) both. People who say they've never had a crush—unrequited, maybe, but in any case not acted upon—are possibly insane on top of it. But if I had any doubts that timing plays a major role in how you feel about a book, this past month put those doubts to rest. As a younger unmarried woman, and at a less settled time in my marriage, I would have wept over Anna's frustration and identified with Emma's covetousness. I would not have spent two minutes thinking about Kitty and Levin, the two characters in *Anna Karenina* whose relationship is in direct opposition—it's careful and slow and cerebral—to Anna and Vronsky's. But these days I read both books the way I sometimes watch horror movies late at night on cable. I get agitated when the hero or heroine starts walking into the house that everybody else has known for hours is haunted. "Don't go there!" I want to shout to Anna and Emma. "This way lies madness. And death."

It's not that I don't know temptation or sympathize with it. A male friend of mine was so lovesick last year for a woman who was not his wife—and with whom, he swears, nothing ever "happened"—that when I found him in tears on September 11, I panicked. Had his wife or kids been at or near the World Trade Center, I asked, nervously, over the phone. No, no, no, he told me, everybody was "fine." It was just that the woman he loved from afar, with whom he was supposed to have lunch that day, was stranded in another city and wouldn't be able to get back for their rendezvous. He was admitting this to me, he said, because he knew I wouldn't "judge" him.

When the whole Bill Clinton–Monica Lewinsky mess exploded, I remember telling a friend that I thought Bill just "couldn't help it." "Oh, he can help it all right," my friend replied sourly. "He just doesn't want to."

As for myself, here's a story: Once upon a time, I met a man, let's call him V., who was everything I thought I'd always wanted: he was charming, he was beautiful, he was wild and impetuous and crazy, mostly about me. Like Anna for a while, I resisted, though given that this was the late twentieth century and not the nineteenth, I was able to manufacture enough socially acceptable situations in which I could test that resistance. To say I was lovesick is a grand understatement; it was as if I had a terminal illness. You know how bodice-rippers always say things like "Every waking hour was consumed by thoughts of . . . him"? Well, every waking hour was consumed by thoughts of him. In fact, thinking back, I can't remember how I managed to keep myself dressed and fed, and away from those open cellar-door things Leo would come along later to scream at me about.

To give you some idea of just how far gone I was, let me tell you this: I didn't read a thing. For months. I couldn't concentrate. And when I did get dragged out—usually by a well-meaning friend to a movie or a play or a dinner—I was incredibly preoccupied. I remember going with my friend Judy to some Woody Allen movie that was supposed to be a comedy, except I came out of it in tears. "What's up with you?" she asked. "I don't know," I lied. "It just seemed so sad. All these people who are in love with the wrong people and not being able to get the 'right' people to love them back," I finally told her. "It's as if he were writing this movie about me." Being a good friend—and, I think, mightily concerned for my mental health—Judy didn't mention that it was perhaps possible that Woody Allen, who would eventually leave Mia Farrow for her adopted daughter Soon Yi, was merely, as usual, writing about himself.

In Tolstoy's world, there are two kinds of relationships: those based on passion and longing like Anna and Vronsky's, and those that exist on more rational, practical terms, like the union struck by Levin and Kitty. In our world, the same is true, except that since we can wait a lot longer to marry and can have plenty of adventures first, it's generally expected that a young woman can get her Vronsky period over with, say, in her early twenties, and then be free to make a "smart" marriage a bit later on. But me, I couldn't seem to get enough of Vronsky-like characters, much to my parents' and even my friends' chagrin. "He's so exciting," I'd say about this or that Vronsky of the moment. "He's so interesting." That whoever-he-was was almost always also extremely difficult—and that whatever relationship we were able to forge was thus extremely explosive—went without saying.

And then I met Leo, who seemed right from the start a perfect blend of the two extremes. On the one hand, he was so different from anybody else I'd known that the whole idea of the relationship was dramatic; that he also has a wildly passionate artistic temperament made him all the more appealing to a woman with a jones for Vronskys. But he was also a seasoned adult, a grown-up, who'd already been married and was insistent that this time around he was going to do it right. As you know, we met in a bar, courtesy of his brother Jim and lots of advance publicity. What you don't know yet is that it was love—or at least attraction—at first sight. Although today he'll tell you that he thought I was "odd" because I was wearing ropes and ropes of fake pearls and a paisley miniskirt, he must have liked me, because he asked me for my number, called me the very next day, and made a date for the following week. The rest happened fast. I can remember everything about those early weeks, right down to the outfit I was wearing (a gray agnès b. skirt, white T-shirt, white Keds: already his minimalist taste was rubbing off on me) on the steamy June night that we declared our love for each other. It was a heady, passionate time, and it seemed to me (as it has seemed to young women in love since time immemorial) that love, passionate love, had indeed conquered all.

In the introduction to the Modern Library edition of *Anna* that I read, the novelist Mona Simpson talks about her reaction to the book, which she read in her twenties. Had I read it at that age, I surely would have believed, as she did, that Anna and Vronsky were "right" to do what they did and that the disasters that befell them were due to the fact that the society in which they lived didn't understand love and was just plain repressive to women. I would have ranted and raved that passion should trump intellect every time and that anyone who doesn't follow her heart at every given moment is "settling," which was the dirtiest word I could ever have used back then. If I had even noticed that there was a subplot about another couple—Levin and Kitty—I would have dismissed it as so much boring old bourgeois nonsense. "They're just counterpoint," I would have said, meaning that they were there only to underscore the great grandness that was Anna and Vronsky.

But I didn't read *Anna Karenina* then, I'm reading it now, and now—fourteen years later, sitting on my lounge chair looking out at the very romantic ocean—I see a completely different book. Suddenly, all the passion and torture that goes on between Anna and Vronsky, and all the disaster they incur, seems so pointless and silly to me: Even a blind person, or one who has lived in a cave all these years and has no idea how *Anna Karenina* will end, can see that Vronsky, for Anna, spells doom.

So I guess I'm just lucky that I was wrong about Leo, that he really wasn't Vronsky at all—or that his Vronskyisms are, I could say, leavened by Levin. While Anna and Vronsky's relationship deteriorates over the years—partly because the Russian society is bent on punishing Anna, but also because a passion like theirs cannot live forever—ours has actually gotten better. In fact, sitting here reading as he sits on the next chair leafing through the *New York Post*, I realize that for all my intermittent frustrations with him, and the occasional blowups worthy of any Russian novel, we've actually been having a good year and that we keep having better years as we both get older and more tired and run out of energy to try to change, as they say in twelve-step programs, the things about each other we cannot change. I've more or less made my peace with the fact that he's socially awkward and, more important, uninterested, and that his default personality position, his toggle switch, is stuck on "grumpy." He seems to have made his peace, more or less, with whatever faults he imagines that I have.

Which is not to say I don't occasionally find myself in medias crush or that I don't long to have the delicious torture of a forbidden life. I miss secrecy and longing and anxiety: all the newness and unknownness and drama that are at the basis of adultery, whatever the time or place. I found myself growing weepy one insomniacal night recently when, for a change, I flipped on the TV and discovered some old French movie in which Gérard Depardieu's wife discovers that he is having an affair with a neighbor. "I'm so jealous!" she screams at him. (Of course, it sounds so much less hackneyed in French.) He nods, assuming she's talking sexual jealousy. "I hate that you've had all those wonderful stolen moments and those secrets," she explains.

I'm not sure that had Leo been awake and watching this with me he would have understood what was happening, or why I was crying. He's way too Levin for that. But while his obliviousness to the subtlety of emotion is one of his traits that drives me craziest, I also realize that it is exactly the trait that has allowed me to have my own secret life, the one that takes place in my library at dawn or in the subway at rush hour or on this very deck where he sits beside me. He thinks of my compulsive reading and writing as "work" and he doesn't much quiz me on it; I'm not about to tell him that I am, just like Anna and Emma, an adulteress. My books are my secret lovers, the friends I run to to get away from the daily drudgeries of life, to try out something new, and yes, to get away, for a few hours, from him. He doesn't need to know that my books are the affairs I do not have.

September 1

Acknowledge This!

You know you're in a bad patch when the most interesting part of the book you're reading is the acknowledgments page.

On one sleepless night last week, I picked up *Girls' Poker Night*, an upscale *Bridget Jones's Diary* about a smart, and smart-talking, New York woman who has more of a lifestyle than a life, and who can't seem to get past her emotional "issues" to have a decent relationship with an actual, real live man.

So far, so ordinary. I almost fell right back to sleep.

But then I flipped to the page that now appears in the front, or occasionally at the back of most books written these days: the acknowledgments page. That's where I read the aforementioned interesting fact. "For his help early in my career," it said, "I am especially grateful to Dave Letterman." The fact that the author, Jill A. Davis, used to work for the late-night comedian is the main thing that differentiates her book from all the others in the genre known as chick lit.

Noticing Davis's employment history didn't make me like the book any more than I did in the first place, but it did help me understand how it got published. She has experience, albeit in another medium. She has a track record. She has, as they might say in Publishing 101, connections, connections, connections.

Here's what book industry insiders routinely use the acknowledgments pages for:

1. To inform or remind them of who the author's agent is, in the event that they're editors and want to know whom to call to get a look at the author's other work, or, if they're agents, to know from whom to steal the author away.
2. To identify the author's specific editor and then surmise how much actual editing might have been done.
3. To check the spelling of the author's family's and friends' names in the event that there will be enough boldfaced names to warrant a book party.

Here's what the average reader can use acknowledgments pages for:

1. To establish how the author did his/her research on the project. A nonfiction exposé may list a lot of attorneys or government types; a biography should indicate which of the subject's family and friends were willing to speak— and thus why, in most cases, those people's quotes are

unfailingly laudatory; a good family drama will surely include the names of the author's spouse and kids.

2. To track an author's romantic or marital history. (NB:
   Sometimes you also need to check the dedication page
   for this.) I was a huge fan of the writer Caroline Knapp,
   author of *Drinking: A Love Story* and *Pack of Two*. When
   Knapp died (at forty-two!) her *New York Times* obituary
   reported that she'd just gotten married the month before. I didn't know Knapp, but I loved *Drinking* so much
   that I felt like I did, and so I wondered: Who was this
   husband, of whom I didn't remember her writing? It
   turned out that he was one of the dedicatees in *Drinking*
   and acknowledged high up in *Pack of Two*.

3. To see if the author has any friends with recognizable
   names, which you can then check against the blurbs on
   the jacket to see if there's been any of what *Spy* magazine used to call "logrolling in our time."

You can save yourself a lot of time and money if you read the
acknowledgments first: they can serve as a little window into the
story you're about to pay your twenty-plus bucks for. Or as the author Stanley Bing puts it, "I like acknowledgments. They give the
reader a taste of the book and get them into it without putting too
much pressure on them."

You like cool, ironic detachment? Start with the introduction
to Dave Eggers's *A Heartbreaking Work of Staggering Genius*. You
like your satire gentle and tongue-in-cheek? Check out Bing's anti-

acknowledgment in his anti-business book *What Would Machiavelli Do?* "I'd also like to acknowledge the enormous contribution of my wife and kids to the general framework of my personal and professional life, but what kind of mean guy would do a thing like that?" You want careful? Flip back a couple of pages and note that I thanked just about every human being I'd met since seventh grade, partly because they each really, truly helped me, but also just in case my naming them might make them feel guilty enough to go out and buy this book.

No wonder acknowledgment pages sometimes go on for chapters and preoccupy writers almost as much as the ranking system on Amazon.com. I know one author, in fact, who opens a Thank You file whenever he begins work on a new book and adds names to it throughout the sometimes years-long process, so concerned is he that he'll leave somebody out. Did writers of previous generations worry like this? Somehow I doubt it. Did Malcolm X (or Alex Haley, with whose "assistance" his *Autobiography* was written) thank the brothers who'd helped him in his life and work? Did Philip Roth thank Portnoy's mother? Did Emily Brontë thank her sisters? Of course not. Maybe in those psychologically naïve days, authors weren't aware of how much the sometimes passive contributions of others helped them to pursue their dreams.

Or maybe they were just a lot less cynical about what interests a reader about a book.

September 11
Oh, God

W ill I ever see, or think, or write that date casually? I won't go into detail about where I was a year ago when I found out about the terrorist attacks, not because it wasn't harrowing but because just about every piece of journalism published the week after 9/11 began with just that kind of "I was brushing my teeth, headed out for a normal day" disclaimer. Since this is a memoir of reading, I've been racking my brain trying to remember what I was reading that day or week, but I'm blank. All I know is that whatever it was, I stopped reading it, and like most of the rest of this city—and some of the country—I spent the following days watching television and "reading" only the newspaper and the occasional newsmagazine account of the disaster. It was hard to concentrate even on those. A few days later, I got a call from a friend who publishes a newsletter; she asked me to recommend books that would somehow explain what had happened, or provide comfort or wisdom.

I remember telling her I'd been thinking a lot about *House of Sand and Fog*, Andre Dubus III's brooding novel about an Iranian general trying to build a postrevolutionary life in southern California; I remembered it as a book about retaining your dignity and about what it means, both good and bad, to be an American. It wasn't about terrorism or religious fundamentalism, and it wasn't hokey like the number-one bestseller on Amazon at the time, *Nostradamus*. It also didn't have any "advice" for surviving post-9/11 trauma. But it was the only book that kept reappearing in my mind.

In the throes of the worst political and social disaster my generation had ever known, in the midst of the biggest news story of the age, I was thinking about a made-up story on a tangential topic by a relatively unknown writer.

How typical. When my father was dying, I remember, I spent hours sitting on the deck outside of his bedroom at home reading T. C. Boyle's *East Is East*, a dark but comic novel about a Japanese sailor shipwrecked at an American writer's colony. Throughout my pregnancy with Charley, when well-meaning friends would pass along their dog-eared copies of *What to Expect When You're Expecting* or Penelope Leach's *Your Baby and Child*, I'd dutifully pile them up on the coffee table—and go on reading the collected works of Philip Roth.

I wasn't then, and I'm not now, looking for escape, exactly. (If I were, I'd have been loading up on mysteries or romances or something.) But what I've come to realize is that I like to take my information in a more impressionistic way. If I'd thought about it—which I didn't—I guess I would have said that *East Is East* was illustrating what I suspected I would soon be feeling—adrift and unprotected in a strange new world—and that Roth's books, about family and Jewishness, were completely appropriate preparation for the birth of my child. It wasn't, obviously, that I didn't care about the processes, or the sciences, of birth or death, but I didn't want to read about them, at least not in the straightforward, linear way that a book about dying or birthing would surely have to be read.

But back where I come from—college, journalism, the world of supposed "ideas"—novels still evoke a faint whiff of disapproval, as if they're the kind of thing that only idle ladies who stay in bed all day and eat bonbons should read. There's also something vaguely sexist about this attitude—women can't handle anything too serious—which is still sneakily pervasive. (Men read novels, too, of course, but the stereotypical "guy's book"—think Tom Clancy— has no moniker akin to the offensive "chick lit.") Nonfiction books routinely sell more copies than fiction, for example, and thus generally earn their authors higher advances. A college professor who publishes a novel may be envied, but it's his colleague with the published nonfiction thesis who's more likely to get tenure. The fiction/nonfiction split in perception is like Woody Allen's stated desire in making *Interiors*, his first serious movie. He wanted to "sit at the grown-ups' table," he famously said. Comedy, like novels, is childish; drama and nonfiction are adult. But have you ever noticed that the highest praise heaped on a book of nonfiction is that it "reads like a novel"?

Although I don't agree that a novel, a good novel, isn't as instructive about the world as any work of journalism, I still feel conflicted. I admit that it has begun to worry me, when I look back on the pages in this journal, that no matter what books I put on my original list of must-reads, no matter how "important" or "relevant" the nonfiction titles I've written there are, the books I reach for again and again are novels. Still, when I ask friends for recommendations, I often get back nonfiction ideas. "Try reading Karen Armstrong's *Islam* or David Fromkin's *A Peace to End All Peace*," an acquaintance from the gym told me last week when I asked for September 11–appropriate fare. And I want to read them, really I do—I usually trot off dutifully to the store or the Internet to buy them. But I've noticed that when an envelope full of nonfiction arrives at my house, it often sits on the coffee table for three or four days. When I know there's a novel inside, I don't even wait to find the scissors, I just tear open the package with my bare hands.

In a recent *New Yorker* article about the author William Gaddis, Jonathan Franzen defines two "models" of reading. The one he calls the "status" model holds that books are works of art and "if the average reader rejects the work it's because the average reader is a philistine." In fact, a book has more status—and thus, apparently, more value—if it's difficult or slow and thus turns most people off. The other kind, Franzen writes, is the contract model, in which the author and the reader tacitly agree that the "deepest purpose of reading and writing . . . is to sustain a sense of connectedness, to resist existential loneliness." Contract readers (and writers) exist on a plane of "pleasure and connection." On careful reading, I realized that Franzen was talking here exclusively about fiction, but the categories he constructs seem to break down for me along fiction and nonfiction lines. My first reaction to a work of nonfiction is to see it as difficult, or at least didactic—homework, in other words. But I approach a novel, no matter how difficult or sophisticated or "literary," as a form of "pleasure and connection."[4]

So maybe that's why, on the September 11 anniversary, the last thing I wanted to do was study something about terrorism or religion or Mideast relations. Those of us living within a mile of Ground Zero had gotten a pretty complete education in those subjects over the past year from both the news programs we'd been watching incessantly and, simply, from just living here. We aren't—or at least I'm not—in the mood for anything hard, or "status-y." In fact, if there was anything even vaguely "good" about the whole experience, it was the sense of connection most New Yorkers felt, and continue to feel, with one another and with Americans in other cities and towns who, up until now, didn't have much use, let alone sympathy, for us in the first place. I wanted to further that sense of what Franzen would call the contract. I wanted a novel.

Still, I did take my gym friend's suggestion and start on *Islam*, which I found fascinating. Within five minutes, I learned that the prophet Mohammed was almost a feminist, preaching long and loudly that women should not be mistreated but cherished. But a weird thing kept happening as I read: when I'd put the book down

---

[4]You may have noticed that nowhere in this discussion, and nowhere in this book, do I opt to pick up a book of poetry, a fact for which I feel mildly guilty, especially since both my mother and my sister have written in that form and I've published a couple of translations. In fact, it's coming back to me that I did read some poems by Stephen Spender around the time of the terrorist attacks, and there was one particular verse from the work of W. H. Auden that was making the e-mail rounds. But even more than nonfiction, poetry seems "homework" to me. Intellectual laziness or product of the typical American education? You decide.

around the house for a minute, to answer the phone or fix some lunch, I'd then be unable, for hours at a time, to find it. The same thing happened with *Germs*, the book that was published right as the anthrax scares began. Instead, I went back to *House of Sand and Fog* and read again about how difficult it is for a Middle Eastern immigrant to reconcile his life in the old world with life in the new. I also, on Liza's recommendation, picked up Jennifer Egan's *Look at Me*, which, before September 11, I would have thought was "just" a novel about a vain model whose face was destroyed in a car accident; now, the subplot—about a Middle Eastern man who lived among Americans for years as a way to learn how best to terrorize them—seemed to take center stage. That's the other thing about a good novel: depending on your state of mind, and even the state of the world, you can probably find at least one of any number of themes to provide you the sense of connection you crave.

Not that you could necessarily explain just why a certain book called to you at any given time or that the relationship between what's going on in your head and what's on the page is necessarily a transparent one. My friend Jim, at the magazine, just told me today that he was at a similar loss for what to read during this emotional week, and that he, too, felt a pull toward fiction. But what fiction? It turns out, he said, that he burrowed down for several days with *The Brothers Karamazov*, even if he wasn't at first sure exactly why. What do you think that has to do with the September 11 anniversary, I wanted to know. "I don't know," he told me. "But it just seemed right. It is, after all, about God and the Devil."

September 18
Kid Stuff

C harlotte's Web is one of those children's books that adults have strong memories of. A woman I know told me the other day that thirty years later, she still tears up at the memory of her mother weeping as she read the book aloud to my friend and her sisters. Another friend told me she used to get into a fight with her younger brother and then purposely run upstairs to read the end of the book so she would burst into tears and then would blame her brother. Another has said that she was shocked to discover, a week before her wedding, that her husband-to-be had never read the book that she felt explained "everything" about her; she told him that his completion of the novel was a requirement for their marriage.

So when I told some friends—parents, most of them—that *Charlotte's Web* would be my book of the week, now that it had turned up on Charley's required third-grade reading list, their eyes welled up. "Oh, it's a great book," they said. "What a great thing to read with your kid." What followed were the inevitable reminiscences of their own read-aloud experiences, their memories of giggling along at the wordplay of Dr. Seuss stories as Mom read the rhymes faster and faster, their eyes and minds opening to the gorgeous, complex and joyous world of being read to.

Except—and here's a confession to mobilize the perfect-mother police—I didn't experience much pleasure at reading aloud, either as a parent or a kid. I wasn't a particularly good or happy participant, then or now, and nobody in either of my families seemed to like it all that much.

I have exactly one memory of reading with my parents, but it's a powerful one. It was the summer before first grade, I think, and my father, who was, to put it mildly, not a get-down-on-the-floor-with-the-kids type of dad, sat with me on the back steps of our house at Harvey's Lake and taught me to read. The book was one of the Dick and Jane series (he must have found it in Liza's or Kuff's room, or on the old creaky shelves). I can see him sitting there in his madras bermuda shorts with his knees up practically under his chin—his legs were so long!—and teaching me to sound out words. "See Jane run," I can hear him saying. "Now you say it."

What I don't remember—or didn't have—is the kind of experiences other people wax rhapsodic about, like rainy afternoons huddled under blankets with Mom, hearing her act out all the different characters in books about Alice and Pippi and Stuart. "Did you guys ever read to me?" I asked my mother on the phone last night. "Well, sure," she replied, but then couldn't name more than one book, *Lucky Little Rabbit*, about which we remember nothing except the fact that I could never pronounce the L's in the titles correctly. "Well, I guess not so much," she finally admitted. "I couldn't stand most of the books," she said. "And then, when you could read to yourself, you did."

In fact, I don't have a lot of memories of so-called children's books at all: I must have read *The Wizard of Oz* and *Stuart Little*—and *Charlotte's Web*, for that matter—but whatever associations I have with them come from the movies. (Pippi Longstocking is another story: I loved the series and can still see the Astrid Lindgren books lined up on my pink-flowered bedroom shelves.) I never read *Lord of the Rings*, having waded through *The Hobbit* (probably a school assignment) with only marginal engagement.

And now, in a cruel but predictable twist of fate, I'm seeing the same behavior in my son. With the exception of the Captain Underpants series, books don't call to Charley. And through most of his first seven years, our nightly read-aloud ritual was more chore than joy. Are my own mother and I the only ones who found reading *The Runaway Bunny*, about the baby rabbit who can never get away from his mother, repetitive and tiresome? Am I the only parent who regularly skipped the middle sections of those interminable Budgie books, until, at about four, Charley began to notice and call me on it? As for Harry Potter, we did pretty well with the first one, but by volume 4, I was hoping somebody'd put a spell on me. I was always too tired or impatient to relax into the process and he too keyed up to concentrate. When it came to bedtime reading, my son and I have long been at cross-purposes: my agenda was to read something quick and easy and get to lights-out; his was to ask for the longest, most complex book, the better to delay it. As a parental reader, I relapse into White Rabbit syndrome. I'm more interested in what reading aloud can accomplish than in what pleasures it can provide.

Obviously, I have complicated feelings about this. On the one hand, I managed to grow up into a reasonably sane adult who undeniably loves reading without a lot of the aforementioned beautiful childhood read-aloud experiences, so it's possible, even likely, that Charley might, too. On the other hand, like most yuppie parents, I feel a pull to right the (perceived) wrongs of my own childhood, to be a better parent than my own perfectly decent ones. Besides, I'd rather he have more to wax rhapsodic about than the video games of his youth and, only if I'm very lucky, all those evenings he and I have spent dancing together in the living room to old Beatles songs.

So *Charlotte's Web*—along with *Charlie and the Chocolate Factory* and the *Just So Stories*—provided an opportunity for both Charley and me. These were the three books Charley chose from his reading list, books which, he informed me, he had to read by himself. Feeling guilty—as if the school *knew* how bad I was at this—I said we'd have to establish our own, different kind of reading ritual. From now on, I told him, we'd read as a tag team: he'd read a chapter, I'd read it right after him—both of us silent, on his bed—and then we'd discuss it.

Charlotte's Web, as any third-grader can tell you, is the story of a pig named Wilbur who is on his way to the slaughter by his farmer/owner until Fern, the farmer's daughter, rescues and befriends him. Banished to a neighbor's barn, Wilbur grows up among the animals, one of whom—Charlotte, the spider—teaches him to believe in himself as a terrific and "radiant" pig. Wilbur becomes the prize animal of the county fair, which assures him a place in history; but even fame and security can't change the inevitable. Soon, Wilbur loses his friend and mentor, Charlotte, to the spider's life cycle. He lives beyond her, but he never forgets her.

I knew the general plot before we started, and frankly, I was a little worried. It sounded awfully bucolic and, well, sweet. I'm a city girl through and through, and stories about farms generally don't do it for me. I know adult titles like Jane Smiley's *A Thousand Acres*, Kent Haruf's *Plainsong*, and Leif Enger's *Peace Like a River* were critically acclaimed and/or bestsellers, but I always have to force myself to read them, so slow and distant do they seem. As for sweet . . . well, like *The Mary Tyler Moore Show*'s Lou Grant, who once told Mary she had spunk and "I hate spunk," I have a problem with it. What if I hated *Charlotte's Web*? What if Charley approached it with the same prejudices? (Worse, what if he loved it and immediately wanted to move to a farm?) I mean, I knew the book was a parable—I'm not that out of it—but I wasn't sure that Charley would get it.

In the days that followed, I came to see that even a beginning reader—or at least my beginning reader, at this stage of his development—approaches a text with the same sort of expectation and demand all the rest of us do. And Charley, despite the weeks he loves spending on Liza's farm amid her bevy of horses, dogs, and cows, is about as drawn to country tales as I am. His initial reaction to the first chapter: "I don't like it, Mom," he said. "It's about a girl and a pig. Why should I care?"

Oh, boy, I thought, here we go: another generation of Nelson readers shunning bucolic childhood classics. "Try reading a little more," I said, hopefully.

The next two nights weren't much better, as E. B. White laid out the rural particulars. ("The barn was very large. . . . It smelled of the perspiration of tired horses.") Don't these descriptions remind you of Aunt Liza's farm? I asked him.

(I was trying hard.)

"I guess," came the bored reply.

I started thinking we should have begun with *Charlie and the Chocolate Factory*. It might be about a candy company owner, but at least there's nothing else sweet about it.

But then, when Charlotte appeared, so did a miracle. "Can we read two chapters tonight?" Charley asked me as soon as Wilbur had met the spider and had a very human reaction to her. "Charlotte is fierce, brutal, scheming, bloodthirsty—everything I don't like," White has Wilbur think. But then, the author explains, "Wilbur was merely suffering the doubts and fears that often go with finding a new friend."

"Sure, Charley," I said. "How come?"

"I like this book now," he said. "The animals are like people, Mom," he replied, with the unspoken "Du-uh" even elementary schoolers have perfected. "They're like kids I know."

For the next few nights, we talked about Templeton, Wilbur, Charlotte, the goose, and the gander more heatedly and more often than we discussed the actual humans in the book. When we looked at the reading form and saw that he was to name the "most interesting" character, he didn't hesitate. "I pick Templeton," the gluttonous rat, he told me. Why? "Because he reminds me of R———," he answered, naming a kid with whom Charley has his first love/hate relationship. "He's funny, but he's mean, too. He only cares about himself." (Or as Charlotte says, "You know how he is—always looking out for himself, never thinking of the other fellow.") When we got to the next to last chapter, in which Charlotte dies, Charley didn't miss a personifying beat: "You know what makes me really sad about this?" he asked. "This line: 'No one was with her when she died.'" He waited a beat and then asked about the only dead person he knows anything about. "Was Poppop alone when he died?"

If it hadn't fully occurred to me before, it did now: even an eight-year-old wants to read about what he knows, to have his own world explicated for him. And if a book is good enough, the venue and the biological classification of the characters don't matter much. This, of course, is the reason *Charlotte's Web* is a classic, and why everybody in the world except me and maybe my brothers and sister remembers it so clearly and so fondly. It is not just about "a girl and a pig," or just about life on a farm; as Eudora Welty wrote in *The New York Times Book Review* in 1952, it's about "friendship on earth, affection and protection, adventure and miracle, life and death, trust and treachery, pleasure and pain and the passing of time."

"So who was your favorite character, Mom?" Charley asked me when we'd finished.

"I think Charlotte," I said.

"That figures," he replied. "She's sort of like you."

Deep in my heart, I'd hoped he'd say that. I secretly thought of myself as Charlotte, especially when I read White's epitaph for her: "It is not often that someone comes along who is a true friend and a good writer. Charlotte was both." Could it be that my son also believed these things about me?

"Yeah? Why do you think so?" I was fishing.

"Well," he said seriously, "she's a girl, but she's still sort of nice. And also, she's really, really bossy."

Finally, we've both got a *Charlotte's Web* memory to wax rhapsodic about.

September 25

Sex and the City

I'm reading a dirty book," I wrote, in Instant Messenger, to my friend Ralph across town.

"Is it hot? Do you like it?" he IMed me back.

A fair question, but one I didn't quite know how to answer. I was sitting in my office at the magazine, feet up on the desk, leafing through *The Sexual Life of Catherine M.*, a memoir that apparently has been all the rage in France and was on its way to bestseller lists here. ("An epic new sex memoir . . . is keeping the French up late," announced *Vogue.*) By page 30, author Catherine Millet had participated in several orgies, announced her nearly exclusive interest in anal sex, and done it outdoors a couple of times. I've barely, uh, penetrated the book but by now I'm kind of bored and Catherine should rightfully have contracted repetitive stress disorder.

But I'm nothing if not a trouper, so I decide to persevere. Maybe the reason the book is leaving me cold, I think, is that I'm reading it under the wrong circumstances. Sitting fully clothed, surrounded by a few dozen chic female colleagues going about the business of putting out a women's magazine is hardly conducive to sexual stimulation. Better to take the book home, put it on the bedside table, and wait for insomnia to strike. Maybe I'll have a different reaction at three A.M. while all cozy in my bed, my sleeping husband at my side.

So that's what I did. ("What are you doing?" Leo asked groggily as I turned on the light. "Oh, reading a sex book," I told him, hoping to tantalize with understatement. "Oh," he said as he fell back to sleep.) Still nothing. By six A.M., I was propping Millet's confessional up on the StairMaster and climbing away. Any sweating or heavy breathing came from the Pro Climber, not the writer's prose.

So no, I would have to tell Ralph later, *The Sexual Life of Catherine M.* is not hot, and I'm not sure I like it. But then maybe it isn't supposed to be. Millet is a French art critic, and she couches her tales of exploits in a kind of Gallic philosophizing we Americans might rename rationalizing. "I am docile," she says, stepping back from a long description of a not completely consensual blow job to write, "not because I like submission . . . but out of a deep-seated indifference to the uses to which we put our bodies." It's passages like this that suggest Millet's intention is for provocation of the intellectual, not the sexual, kind.

The cerebralizing of sex has been done before, many times, of course, but the title that Millet's reminds me of, suddenly, is Richard Rhodes's *Making Love*, a clear-eyed 1992 memoir in which the author meticulously recounts his sex life, complete with his total number of partners (a surprisingly low eleven for someone who lived through the sexual revolution), the length of his erect penis (five and a half to six and a half inches, depending whether you're measuring along the top or the underside), and long, detailed descriptions of his efforts to bring his wife to orgasm. While Catherine M. has more narrative thrust, shall we say, than Rhodes's treatise, they're both strangely distant from their subject matter, overly concerned with numerology (Millet seems obsessed with counting partners, orgasms, everything up to ants on the ground or cracks in the ceiling) and, well, dull.

But there's also one important difference between the two. When *Making Love* came out, nobody went around calling it erotica. It wasn't and it didn't pretend to be. But Millet's confessional—which is published by Grove Press, the house known for works by Henry Miller, Anaïs Nin, et al.—on the other hand, seems to be trying to hedge its bets. Like everybody, Millet has her sexual tropes—two or three activities she really likes—and if you're lucky enough to share her taste, you might get turned on. But if you don't—and who is totally, completely, and continuously in sync with another person's sexuality?—you can at the very least admire the author's unflinching honesty. (It's not easy, I'd guess, to commit to paper the fact that one likes to be forced into fellatio, or gets off on groups of men lining up and screaming abuse at one another while waiting their turns, or finds something particularly appealing about extremely dirty—as in unwashed—partners.) And if all else fails, there's the philosophizing to keep you warm at night.

I wouldn't know how to begin discussing the difference between erotica and pornography, and minds far greater than mine have analyzed the philosophy of sex, but as the old saying goes: I know what I like. And it seems that what's out there advertised as "sexy" isn't it.

Take Susan Minot's *Rapture*, for example, a novel that takes place during one illicit act of fellatio. It's listed on Amazon.com under erotica; in fact, on the day I looked, it was the only novel in the top ten. (The others were increasingly specific collections; had I continued on through all four dozen listings, I'm pretty sure I would have discovered the ultimate in niche marketing: a book, say, for left-handed hermaphrodite lesbian cross-dressers who own dogs.) The problem is, there is nothing sexy about the book, which in fact reads more like *The Girls' Guide to Hunting and Fishing* than *Fanny Hill*. The engaged-to-be-married man and the fellating woman scan back through their memories of their relationship and banally ponder questions of attraction, commitment, and loss—and once every few pages (the book, mercifully, has only 115 of them), Minot offers up a tiny detail about the act they're engaging in.

This is sexy? I don't think so.

So I'm frustrated, in more ways than one, and decide to ask friends about their erotic favorites. Not a one mentions *Rapture* or *Catherine M*. Nicholson Baker's *Vox* gets tapped, but mostly, I think, because it's a title people know, thanks to Monica Lewinsky having given it to Clinton. (No one—and I've talked to dozens of people, most of them avid readers—even mentions Baker's execrable *The Fermata*, which made *Vox* look like *Rebecca of Sunnybrook Farm*.) I was amazed at the number of people who immediately blurted, "Page 28 in *The Godfather*" (mass-market paperback edition), and even more amazed that I knew, immediately, just what scene they meant. (You know: Sonny and the bridesmaid doing it against the bedroom door as the wedding is starting downstairs.) My friend Mark chose a story called "Innocence" by Harold Brodkey, all about a man trying to give a woman an orgasm (take that, Richard Rhodes!), a couple of people—men, natch—favor Richard Ford. And then there were the middle-aged guys who pointed to the meat-masturbation scene in *Portnoy's Complaint*, and the baby-boomer women who cited the zipless fucks in *Fear of Flying*. One of my friends said, "I have just three words for you: *Lo-li-ta*." Me, I have a strong memory of the toe-sucking scene in *Lloyd*, by Stanley Bing. The image of the heroine, Mona, sitting on a conference table bare-legged—and more important, bare-footed—as her colleague Lloyd tries desperately not to pop her toes in his mouth provokes out-loud laughter, and something more. (It's proof positive, if anyone doubted it, that humor is a necessary component for sex.) Lloyd's tortured fantasy remains such a strong memory that when I expect to see Bing, whom I know socially, I pay careful attention to my footwear.

What I find interesting in all this is that except for a couple of votes for *The Story of O*, the readers I know define as sexy specific scenes from specific works of fiction rather than, say, Nancy Friday's nonfiction fantasy-fest *My Secret Garden; Sex and the City*'s Kim Cattrall and Mark Levinson's recent *Satisfaction*, a manual so explicit it came in a shrink-wrapped bag; or anything labeled erotica or porn. Could it be that what attracts us is the surprise of an unexpected lovemaking scene in an otherwise linear narrative?

Maybe. Or maybe it's that such scenes are what formed our perception of sexy books in the first place.

I once was interviewed for a women's magazine article about the role and importance of alcohol in a college woman's life, and I half-jokingly told the writer that had it not been for drinking, I would never have learned about sex. (She then told me a lot of people had said that.) But the truth is, I owe a lot of the knowledge and appreciation I have for sex to writers and to books, particularly to the late Harold Robbins. In junior high, my best friend Becky and I were *79 Park Avenue* and *A Stone for Danny Fisher* junkies. Every day after school, after we'd put on the stereo and competed to see who could hold the last note in the Jefferson Airplane's "Somebody to Love" as long as Grace Slick did, we'd retire to one or the other of our bedrooms to read from the Robbins oeuvre. We were so committed to the author, in fact, that we each compiled a complete set of the books and kept them in boxes under our beds. That way, we'd always have a sex scene to read, no matter whose house we were visiting.

A lot of people have this kind of sex-scene sense memory. My friend Judy says she used to read and reread a certain breast-fondling scene from *Exodus* and she and her then best friend would go hide in the friend's father's trailer (!) to reread a particularly hot seduction passage from James Michener's *Hawaii*. Even Leo, who as we know is something of a reticent reader, admits he used to carry around a dog-eared copy of Mary McCarthy's *The Group*. A Catholic-school boy all the way through college, Leo kept the book in his knapsack instead of, say, under his bed like the proverbial teenage *Playboy* fan, because that was the one place neither his parents nor the nuns would ever look. Like Becky and me, he had favorite passages, which he marked by turning down the corners of the pages but not, he emphasizes, by writing anything in the margins. That would be too obvious, he explains. Should somebody have found the book, they might have *known* what he was thinking.

In scouting books for the magazine, I recently came upon a new novel, called *The Art of Seeing*, by Cammie McGovern. For the most part, I didn't like it. But I was struck by one aside that comes late in the book, in which the narrator explains that the heroine and her parents often listened to books on tape while riding in the car. It was a great educational and family bonding experience, she says, unless the book they chose happened to have a sex scene.

I can definitely relate. Except for those afternoons with Becky, I don't think I've ever read a favorite sex scene aloud to another person—or had one read to me—and I've never understood the sex-manual advice suggesting that couples should read such passages to each other. Am I prudish about sex? I don't think so. I'd say it's actually a matter of having correctly ordered priorities. The mingling of bodies and emotions and fluids is one thing, I say. But reading about it: now, that's *personal*.

Sex and the City—Across the Pond

I was talking books with Susanna,[5] one of the twenty-somethings who works at the magazine, when I mentioned the novel *Fear of Flying.*

"What's that?" she asked.

"It's a book from the seventies about women and sex that kind of changed the way several generations have relationships," I said, adding that Erica Jong—who coined the term "zipless fuck"—was the first mainstream female writer to talk about sex the way male authors had always done. "You know," I said, "I could probably scare up a copy for you if you want to read it."

"No, thanks," she said. "I don't really read historicals."

There are probably a dozen appropriate responses to that comment—loud guffaws, for example, or a healthy session of eye-

---

[5]A lot of the names I've been using are real, but this one's not. It was changed to protect the ignorant.

rolling—but I was too stunned to make them. *Fear of Flying* is a historical? I thought. Dated, perhaps. A period piece, maybe. But a historical novel? I didn't think so, but I was struck too (uncharacteristically) speechless to respond at all.

Had I been more on top of my game, I might patiently have explained to my friend that a book is not a historical if it takes place in the same era in which it's written. Anita Shreve's *Fortune's Rocks*— about a young woman at the turn of the nineteenth century—is a historical, since it was published in the 1990s (though it's not a particularly good one because all of Shreve's late-nineteenth-century characters have the political agendas of late-twentieth-century ones). Ian McEwan's *Atonement*, about Britain during the Second World War and published in 2002, is a (much better) historical. Jane Austen's books, which were written about and in the same nineteenth-century period, are not, technically speaking, historicals. And neither, of course, is *Fear of Flying*, which is in fact the definition of contemporaneous. In her groundbreaking book, Jong put her finger directly on the tumultuous sex-role-changing era in which she was living.

It's tempting to dismiss Susanna's comments as the simple ignorance of youth or to give in to my favorite pastime: lamenting the lack of education among recent college graduates. (While enjoyable, that isn't really fair, as most students today are not totally responsible for their own literary ignorance. Dissing them is sort of like blaming the victim. If I'd had the opportunity to get four credits for, say, the Semiotics of *Seinfeld* at an accredited institute of higher learning, I too might have chosen that over the complete works of Shakespeare.) But it may be that she simply misspoke, and said "historical" when she really just meant "old books" or "books written about times other than my own."

Take a look at my first appendix again. You'll see plenty of old books there, books like *The Autobiography of Malcolm X*, which I did finally read this year. There were also some bona fide historicals, like *Restoration*, by Rose Tremain, about seventeenth-century England, on the list. But somehow, they're rarely what I reach for first. Like Susanna, I usually don't feel compelled to read about "olden times," preferring to focus on books about "the way we live now," as Trollope once put it. Historical novels all too often read to me like costume dramas or, even worse, foreign movies with subtitles. They're too "arty," they don't seem "real" because the characters speak in a language I don't immediately recognize and understand.

So I was dubious when a friend suggested I read Emma Donoghue's *Slammerkin*. Like Susanna, I immediately felt as though I were getting a history assignment from my eleventh-grade teacher. (The way-too-vague jacket didn't help, either.) But my friend was insistent. "It's not about history," she insisted, and then delivered her knowing punch line: "It's actually about clothes."

Slammerkin is a first novel by thirty-something Donoghue, who is the daughter of Irish literary critic Denis Donoghue. (No offense, Emma, but to us middlebrow Yanks, that could work against you, not for you.) It has all the earmarks of the dreaded you-know-what: it was written in the 1990s (published in 2000), it takes place in eighteenth-century England, and people dress and talk like characters in a Merchant–Ivory film.

It's also a bawdy, funny, captivating read. And my friend was right: it's all about clothes.

"Slammerkin," apparently, is an old English word that can mean either "a loose dress" or "a loose woman," both of which make plenty of appearances in the novel. Mary Saunders is cast out of her working-class London home in 1748 because of her innate love of fashion: she gave her honor in exchange for a traveling salesman's red ribbon. Now "ruined," she has no choice but to become a prostitute along the Dials, sometimes turning as many as a dozen sleazy, perfunctory tricks a night. But Mary has another skill, no less sensually described: "Thread seemed to obey [her]; cloth lay down obediently at her touch." She soon lands a job as an apprentice seamstress to an old friend of her estranged mother, a position that eventually leads to disaster. In the end, the culture condemns her for the one thing she cannot help: she is a woman who loves fashion.

As a woman who loves fashion, I could identify, because if there's one thing I care about as much as my books in the bedside piles and on the cherry shelves, it's the stuff hanging in my closet(s). One of the things I've neglected to tell you is that when in the middle of the night I've pulled all manner of books off the shelves, I often head for the closet to do the same with my clothes. Has this great Calvin Klein suit survived my ten-pound weight gain? Who knew that this old black tunic would come back into style? As surely as I spend many late-night hours asking the world's most important question: What should I read next? I also face the equally pressing one: What shall I wear tomorrow? Like choosing a book, choosing an outfit is, for me, a conscious, deliberate act, one that makes some statement to the world and to myself about how I'm feeling that day. And if my clothes-aholism hasn't brought me to wrack and ruin the way Mary's did, it has provided me with more than a couple of anxious moments, usually just as the truck backs up to my building to deliver my gigantic MasterCard bill.

Donoghue clearly understands the way some women love clothes. *Slammerkin* is filled with luscious passages of the heroine surrounded by brocades and linens and velvets, touching sections of Mary choosing just the right slammerkin for her stroll through the Dials, and myriad scenes in which women bond with their wardrobes. The fabrics and dresses and accessories are so plentiful and so center-stage here that they become characters, as surely as they would a couple of centuries later in *Sex and the City*, which, by the way, addresses many of the very same themes. The lust for beauty, the price of attraction, the way vanity can be your downfall: you can watch them play out on an HBO series or you can read about them in *Slammerkin*. The fact that the book takes place in another century is almost beside the point.

So I loved *Slammerkin* and only wish every historical writer could get completely inside her, um, material the way Donoghue does. I agree with the London *Financial Times* reviewer who said the story never gets "weighted down by its time," and with the jacket copy that brags, "Donoghue wears her learning as lightly and as jauntily as the strolling girls did their slammerkins." It has a lightness despite its serious consequences, and it never becomes didactic or moralistic, like, say, Margaret Atwood's *Alias Grace*, a 1996 novel that may have been inspired by the same historical crime.

When I read that much-praised book, I felt as though I were read-ing about issues and symbols rather than people. I was not a fan.

Like Susanna, I—and most readers—want to read about people who seem real to us, people and situations that in some ways re-flect our life. But Susanna misses the point when she suggests that books written before, say, 1990 can't do that. A good historical is good because it both takes you away from your own circum-scribed world and puts you in the center of it: it shows you that despite the funny clothes, and the unusual language, and the long-gone venues, people are all pretty much the same. The issues that occupy us—issues like jealousy, vanity, and lust, for example—don't change, even if the societies in which we play them out do.

Mary Saunders may have lived in an era when an openly sexual woman was scorned and the punishment for vanity was, literally, death. We may live in a more open-minded society (or maybe not, but that's another story). But a lot of us live by the same rules Mary learned on the the eighteenth-century London streets—"Clothes make the woman. Clothes are the greatest lie ever told."

Hmm. Now that's starting to sound like an idea that even Su-sanna might get. After all, we do all work at a fashion magazine.

"Try this," I think I'll tell her on Monday, as I drop the hard-cover on her desk. "Don't think of it as homework," I'll say. "Think of it as *InStyle*, the eighteenth-century version."

October 10

Afterlife with Father

It wasn't the Kennedy assassination or, God knows, September 11, but I can remember very clearly the first thing I did after reading *The New York Times* one day in November 1986: I picked up the phone and called my father. "Did you see the news about this big insider-trading scandal?" I asked him. "Oh, yeah," he replied. "I always thought those junk-bond guys were lousy crooks!"

A businessman with his own small furniture-manufacturing company, my father, Charles, had never worked on Wall Street, but he was an individual investor, and the stock market was one of our pet topics. As early as grade school, after my mother would drill all four of us kids on spelling words at dinner, my father and I would retire to the living room, where I'd drink Tab and he'd drink Scotch and he'd harangue me—his prized sapphire ring on his amazing long left hand rhythmically tapping the coffee table—about price/earnings ratios and buying on margin.

And I was a willing student. I was interested in math, but even more, I was fascinated by my father, who I literally believed ruled the world. My family still laughs about the time I went to third grade and told everyone that he was now the "president"; he'd been chosen to run a local business association, but in my adoring little-girl way, I'd extrapolated a bit. I thought he had been elected to run the country. While I eventually settled into a slightly more realistic worldview about him, I still continued to look forward to those long evenings when, home from school on vacation, we'd sit—by now I'd join him in the Scotch—and dissect the latest business news. There was something kind of back-room-of-smoky-bar forbidden about our conversations, and I was plenty aware that the fact that he was talking business with me, his younger daughter, was unusual. It made me feel "chosen" and grown-up.

So when I read about the arrest of Ivan Boesky, the star arbitrageur of the 1980s who'd been arrested for insider trading and a host of other crimes, it was only natural that I'd call Charles. And in the months that followed—as more and more brokers, lawyers, and "arbs" were arrested, tried, and sentenced—my father and I reinstated our regular discussions, this time by phone. Was what Michael Milken did worse than what Boesky did? we'd argue. What about that handsome Martin Siegel, the investment banker who got off with a far lighter sentence? Mostly, we'd debate the ins and outs of the cases (as far as either of us could understand them: they were *very* complicated) and discuss the specifics of the insider-trading laws. While we agreed that what most of these guys had done was unconscionable, criminal and just plain "lousy"—my father's favorite word—neither of us was completely convinced that the laws against insider trading, per se, were really enforceable. Isn't it natural, we'd wonder, to want to share information with your family and friends and to protect them from losing their fortunes?

Given all that interest, you would think that I would have been first in line at the bookstore back in 1991 to buy *Den of Thieves*, the meticulous account by *Wall Street Journal* reporter James B. Stewart of the Boesky/Siegel/Levine/Milken cases that led to the late-eighties stock market crash and subsequent recession. But for me, the publication of the book illustrated another aspect of Reading Rule #2: Timing, timing, timing. In this case, bad timing. My father had died just the year before, and while I remained a newshound, some of the thrill had gone out of my Wall Street obsession. There was no one I enjoyed chewing over the business news with, at least not in the same way. So while I must have bought the book—there it was last week, sitting on the cherry shelves—it wasn't until now, when I was coming off yet another birthday and similar but much, much bigger corporate and insider-trading scandals were dominating the news, that I thought to read it.

You know the old expression "The more things change, the more they stay the same"? Well, that's what I'd say about the revelations in *Den of Thieves*, but I'd add one thing: They stay the same, only bigger and badder. Lying on my living room couch all Sunday afternoon as Charley and his best friend Luke played nearby, I found myself chuckling disbelievingly over some of the statistics. Dennis Levine, the first inside trader arrested in the scandal in 1986, had made $12.6 million in illegal profits. In 1984, junk bond king Michael Milken made a total of $23 million. The next year, that handsome Martin Siegel received a $3 million bonus. These are big numbers, obviously, and far more than Charles or I ever had in our collective piggy banks, but by today's standards they seemed like a pittance. I was overcome with a desire to pick up the phone again and call Charles to compare the *Den of Thieves* story with the alleged corruption at WorldCom, Enron, and Martha Stewart. I could almost hear his reaction: "Hey, Saroo, what'd you think? Would Milken's $23 million just about pay for [convicted Tyco honcho] Dennis Koslowski's annual supply of dental floss?"

Oh, Dad, if only I could talk to you about how little and how much things have changed. There's no more World Trade Center, for one thing, which was the scene of some of the crimes discussed in this book. There's also no more Kidder, Peabody, a firm that figured prominently here. Michael Milken has survived both jail and cancer, but he's still a very, very rich man respected for his philanthropy. I know my father would think it as weird as I do to be talking about the late eighties crash that resulted from all these scandals while the TV in the next room is blaring about the recession we're in right now, the one that has caused middle managers to have to forgo retirement while forty-year-old CEOs put their tens of millions into Florida homes that can't be repossessed. If he were here, we'd have a good gallows-humor-type chuckle over the ever-thus nature of the world. I'd tell him about Stewart's assertion, toward the end of the book, that the Milken et al. scandals have "led many to question whether justice was served, and whether future scandals will be deterred." *I can just see you slamming your ring on the table over that one.*

But if the message of *Den of Thieves* is depressing, the experience of reading it now turned out to be anything but, because for three straight nights I lay awake channeling my relationship with my late adored dad. (If reading *Patrimony* reminded me of him, *Den of Thieves* came closer to bringing him back.) "Didja notice," I could imagine myself saying, "that none of the bad guys in this story are women?" (I had a habit, especially in those days, of using just about anything to further my argument that women are, in fact, better human beings than most men.) "Yeah," I can hear him reply. "But what worries me is that so many of the guys are Jewish." (Like a lot of post-WWII Jews, my parents constantly worried that the Christian world looks for a way to blame us for everything.) I'd tell him that I thought it was interesting that John Mulheren, one of Boesky's chums, was tight with no greater a working-class hero than his New Jersey neighbor Bruce Springsteen. "Who the hell is that?" he'd say. Pretty soon, I figured, we'd be off the subject of business and the stock market and *Den of Thieves* altogether. "Have you heard any good jokes lately?" he'd ask, before launching into the kind of vaguely off-color story he loved.

So I guess you could say I had a great week reading *Den of Thieves*, but only partly because it is, as a friend of mine put it the other day, "*the* paradigm of a business book." Some people would say it is an almost mythic morality tale about corruption, punishment, and redemption. But what it made me feel was nostalgic and wistful and sentimental. It reminded me yet again that what's in a book is only part of what matters; in the right circumstances and with the right history, just about any book can take you where you need to go, even if you could never have found that place on a map.

My mother has told me that ever since her mother died, she regularly dreams that the two of them are sitting around talking about the routine events of their lives. This doesn't make her sad, she says; in fact, she usually wakes up refreshed and happy, having felt that she and her mother had a "nice visit." Moralistic and heavy and complicated as it is, *Den of Thieves* did for me what my mother's dreams do for her: it transported me to a dreamlike world, one that I don't get to visit very often anymore. It's a world where a girl and her father sit up long into the night, drinking and arguing and talking about life.

October 24

No Business Like Our Business

When I was in college, and for a few years after, I hung around with a lot of aspiring actors, directors, and playwrights, what we used to call drama folk. Our catchphrase in those days, whenever anybody would mount a production or take a part—let's say, somebody was going to play Hamlet or, this being the eighties, write a Sam Shepardish play—was "the definitive performance has been done." What this meant was that you were risking your creative life to try to re-enact something that had already been done to perfection; there wasn't much chance that any college kid was going to outdo Sir Laurence Olivier, for example, or write a piece that was weirder or more touching than any of Sam's.

That sentence came back to me, loud and clear, this week as I opened books that had come to me at the magazine for possible excerpt or review. On one day, I received two debut novels about the publishing business—one by a guy named Adam Davies, who'd written *The Frog Prince*, about his experiences as an editorial assistant at a book publisher, and the other, Caroline Hwang's *In Full Bloom*, the story of a Korean-American junior fashion editor who's up for a promotion at a *Vogue*-like place just as her mother arrives in town vowing to find her a nice Korean-American husband. A few weeks earlier, I had received, through nefarious and thus undivulgeable methods, a partial manuscript of a novel whose sale had just made waves throughout the fashion magazine business: *The Devil Wears Prada*, it's called, and it's a none-too-nice roman à clef by Lauren Weisberger, a former assistant to Anna Wintour, editor in chief of *Vogue*. This one, in particular, was the subject of a lot of speculation and discussion around the office; although they'd probably have to carry it around in plain brown wrappers, virtually all the staffers in the fashion and beauty end of magazine publishing said they would read the book when it was published.

I've read all three, and while they each have various amusing and/or entertaining things about them, they don't measure up to what I think of as "the original." That book was written by Calvin Trillin and published in 1980. It's called *Floater*.

Floater is about a guy who fills in for vacationing, or otherwise absent, editors at a newsweekly, probably *Time* magazine, at which the author worked early in his career. It's full of characters anybody who has ever worked in this business will recognize: the medical editor who routinely comes down with whatever obscure illness he just reported on, the tipster who is almost always wrong, the stringer who insists that two-thirds stockings for women are a trend but is unable to articulate which part of the leg two-thirds stockings are supposed to cover. The plot—the magazine is trying

to find out whether or not the First Lady is pregnant—is even flim-
sier than the hosiery idea, but it doesn't even matter: Trillin, who
has since written many other books and is now an official "American humorist," is all about character and riff. My favorite is Wolfer-
man's law (named after the staffer who devised it), a theorem that
says the number of extramarital affairs going on in any office always remains constant (sixteen to nineteen couples), as some
adulterers go back to their spouses and others step up to the plate.

People don't talk much about *Floater* these days—I'm such a loy-
alist I'm wounded, on Trillin's behalf, that neither Hwang nor Davies
nor any other latter-day pretenders allude to the Master in their jacket
copy or interviews—but it made a lot of noise in my circle at the time
it was published. Like *Heartburn*, it depicted a world my friends and
I knew a little about and aspired to a lot, and like *Heartburn*, it was
funny and arch and true. In fact, when I reread it this week, and discovered that one of my favorite Trillin lines was missing—I distinctly
remember him once writing that the fee an author gets paid for an
article should always, definitely, exceed the cost of the luncheon at
which the article was assigned—I immediately e-mailed my old
friend Joanne. (Joanne and I became somewhat estranged in the post-
Heartburn days and only now, thanks to the ease and anonymity of
e-mail, occasionally and affectionately communicate.) "Where's the
quote about the cost of the lunch?" I asked her. "Let me search my
Trilliana and I'll get back to you." (See why I liked her so much for so
long? Only Joanne could say "Trilliana" so casually and get away with
it.) Two hours later, the verdict arrived: my favorite line was never in
Floater at all, but in an essay Trillin published in a magazine—it later
turned up in his collection called *Uncivil Liberties*.

The highest compliment anybody ever gave me was that an essay I wrote reminded her of one from the great man's *Alice, Let's Eat;* if that's true, I feel like I could die happy. But somehow, for all that I idolized Calvin Trillin and his work, I never developed Trillin envy anywhere near as intense as what I experienced with dear old Nora Ephron. Why? Partly, I think, because Calvin Trillin is a man, and it's not nice to envy people who have only one X chromosome. Also, from all accounts—and that means from careful readings of virtually all of his books, the lack of gossip within the New York writers' community, and the adorable dedications, almost always to his late wife, Alice—Calvin Trillin is a certifiably nice man. In fact, I recently met him at a book fair at Charley's school. He lives in my neighborhood, and he just happened to have a new book out that he was signing and flogging. He seemed almost shy. "It's nice to meet you, Mr. Trillin," I said to him humbly as he looked down at his shoes. "I'm a big fan, particularly of *Floater.*"

That made him look up.

"*Floater?*" he said, as surprised as if I'd said I was his long-lost child. "Really?"

"I bet you don't hear a lot about *Floater* from people these days," I said. (I was feeling pretty puffed-up, all of a sudden.)

His response was vintage, deadpan Trillin. "I didn't hear a lot about it when it was published," he said.[6]

---

[6]As a meet-your-idol experience, I'd say this one rates pretty high. At least I didn't mumble incoherently, the way I did the one time I met Joseph Heller—what can you say to the guy who invented the concept "Catch-22"?—or the time I was introduced to Arthur Miller. Looking into the face of the creator of *Death of a Salesman,* I could think only two thoughts: (1) Great play! And (2) What was Marilyn Monroe really like?

But even if Trillin's right and most people didn't read, or don't remember, *Floater,* there are an awful lot of unconscious imitators out there. I'm tempted to do a study, in fact, and see how many books about publishing are published every year. Right off the top of my head I can think of *Men in Black,* by Scott Spencer, one of the all-time great novels, about a guy who writes a book under a pseudonym and then has to travel the country promoting it as a person who doesn't exist. And then, of course, there's *Bridget Jones's Diary,* which was almost as much about the writing business as about love and romance.

And of course, this makes sense: many of the people who decide what to publish are frustrated writers themselves, and so they think either everybody else is as fascinated with our silly little business as they are and/or if they themselves ever get it together to write, they should take the advice they've been doling out to wannabe-published authors for years, to "write about what they know." This would explain the seemingly disproportionate number of books about the relatively small book-and-magazine industry; I mean, I don't find a lot of books about truckers landing on my desk. But as magaziney as *Floater* is, its venue is almost beside the point: the book, like all great satires, is about more than the sum of its characters and its admittedly thin plot. I venture to guess that anyone who has ever worked in an office, and that includes an awful lot of readers, would find herself enamored enough of Calvin Trillin's masterwork to do what I did: attach myself to the book (purchased used over the Internet, since it's long out of print) for three nights running and even break the hardcovers-stay-home rule and carry it around in my purse.

But that still doesn't explain why I retain such bonhomie toward Trillin, even if he did sign a copy of *Tepper Isn't Going Out* for me last weekend. Why am I not jealous that he published a novel about our wacky, character-filled business and lived to tell the tale, even if he's right and nobody except me and a couple of my friends have ever heard of it? For a long time I thought I wanted to do exactly the same thing, and for years kept in a drawer an outline for my very own publishing novel. It was about a women's lifestyle magazine at which the health editor was a smoker who regularly took a break at four P.M. to gobble a candy bar, and the fitness expert was a lush whose idea of exercise was lifting a glass of wine to her mouth.

But I never wrote that book, and once I read *Floater*, I knew I never would.

I wasn't envious of Trillin so much as grateful to him. He'd let me off the hook.

After all, the definitive performance had been done.

November 3

Saturdays with Charley

I tend to have a strong negative reaction to people who announce right off the bat that they're contrarians. Contrary to what? I want to ask. I know, I know: they're people who tend to buck the common wisdom, who pride themselves on not running with the pack, who go out of their way to disagree, often simply for the sake of disagreement. These people annoy me because there's something smug about them: Who exactly are they to decide what the common wisdom is, and isn't it just a tiny bit lazy to automatically disagree with it? They remind me of the publishing-course students I used to teach who would come up with ideas for magazines they could describe no more succinctly than to say, "It'll be like *The New Yorker*, only better." That's not an idea, I'd tell them, it's a reaction.

Still, I'm a little bit contrarian on occasion, especially when it comes to books—but then, you already knew that. Obviously, I tend to get my back up when a book is hyped to death, and I have an almost instinctive ability to look at a book everybody else likes and find (or imagine) its flaws. Maybe it's my reporter's background, although people who knew me as a kid say I was always this way. "She's going to be a lawyer," they used to say. "She has an argument for everything." Or as Leo says regularly now, using a metaphor I've never completely understood, "You could talk a peel off a grape."

But I like to think that I'm at least a little more sophisticated than the average contrarian, that on some occasions at least I don't contribute to a backlash so much as begin the backlash to the backlash. Case in point: Now that it has become fashionable, after its enormous success, to dis a book called *The Lovely Bones*, I've become all the more adamant in my praise of it. Likewise, to those revisionists who suggest that Bret Easton Ellis's *American Psycho* is, after all, a great piece of real literature, I insist that it is, as just about everybody said at the time of its publication, a piece of trash.

Last weekend, then, should have been a contrarian's delight. Leo and Charley and I had been invited to visit my dear friend Maria at her lovely hand-restored farmhouse in upstate New York, the kind of trip we rarely make, thanks to Leo's weekend production schedule and my—here it comes—inherent contrarianism. (Why should I drive two and a half hours to look at a tree? I think, remembering my two favorite lines about city folk in the country. "I am at two with nature," Woody Allen once said. A colleague's mother put it this way: "Nature? Who needs it!") But we had a lovely time: Charley played with Maria's daughter, Isabelle, while Leo and T.J. and Maria and I sat around talking and drinking, with the emphasis on the drinking. Several bottles of wine later, I found myself wide awake in Maria's pristine guest bedroom at four A.M., with Charley and Leo by my side. High as we were, Maria—as usual, the perfect hostess—had pressed a book into my hand as I staggered up the stairs a few hours earlier. "I loved this," she said about Mitch Albom's blockbuster inspirational title, *Tuesdays with Morrie.* "I got it from the library."

Five million Americans have read *Morrie*—in hardcover—but up until now I hadn't been one of them. For me, the book had two strikes against it: it is a thousand times too famous (Did you know there is now a play based on it? What's the matter? A major TV movie, produced by Oprah and starring Jack Lemmon, wasn't enough?), and it was a spiritual, inspirational title, which just about never lands in my must-read pile. (The only exception I can think of is *Traveling Mercies*, Anne Lamott's collection of essays on faith; I did read that, and while I found it far less useful than, say, her *Bird by Bird*, even I could appreciate that her faith was completely heartfelt.) But that night, it also had two things going for it: it was short, and thus much more appealing in my tipsiness than the book I'd brought, and most important, Maria had given it to me.

Like Mary, Maria is a relatively new friend; her daughter is in school with Charley, and despite the growing third-grade requirement that boys don't talk to girls or vice versa, the two of them still like to play together. Maria's a fashion designer—she makes spectacular handbags that strangers routinely stop me on the street to ask about—and a smart and thoughtful person. Maria once told me that her favorite author was Anita Brookner, because reading Brookner's small British novels takes her on vacation from the hectic New York life she lives as a businesswoman and mother. She's also the one who told me she read a couple of chapters of the copy of *I Don't Know How She Does It* that I gave her, and then put it aside; like me, she felt it only took a couple of dozen pages to get the gist of the whiny-mother-who-can't-quite-have-it-all novel everybody else is raving about. In other words, I have come to love Maria: she's smart and she doesn't live by the common wisdom. For all that she sometimes disparages herself as conventional and conservative, she never ceases to surprise me. In other words, she's a little bit of a you-know-what, just like you-know-who.

So when I wake up at four A.M., with both Charley and Leo crammed into the antique bed beside me, I pick up *Tuesdays with Morrie* and begin to read. I'm harboring the ultimate contrarian fantasy that it will, like all the best books and friends, turn out to surprise me, and that I'll go home tomorrow brimming with insights about the bestseller that all my snootier book friends have avoided like the plague. I'm hoping I'll be able to tell Maria at breakfast how much I loved the book, and how misunderstood it has been by the so-called intelligentsia, who've embraced the writings of Thich Nhat Hanh, say, but turn their noses up at Morrie Schwartz's and Mitch Albom's homegrown Zen.

But it becomes clear pretty fast that I'm not going to be able to do that. By page 20, I'm simultaneously bored and annoyed. This is the book that sat on the bestseller list for a couple of years, that was made into a very successful TV movie and that has made Mitch Albom one of the most successful journalists of our age? This book, the one that for 192 artless pages extols wisdom that boils down to (a) stop and smell the roses, (b) don't sweat the small stuff, and (c) concentrate not on money or status but on love of family and community? Truthfully, I'm not that surprised by the book's success—the unbearably treacly *Bridges of Madison County* was a megahit and practically spawned its own industry a few years back. I'm more depressed by it. Is it true, as a wise man once said, that you can never go broke underestimating the intelligence of the people? Or worse, am I so out of it, such a snob and so emotionally and spiritually deprived, that I'm missing the point of the book?

Maybe I'm not trying hard enough to identify, I think. A friend who has been in AA tells me that one of the precepts of the program is that you should concentrate on the similarities in the drinking-life stories members tell and forget about the differences. So I try to find points of connection between Albom and me. Let's see: we're about the same age (he was at Brandeis when I was at Yale, at any rate); we're both Jewish (I'm assuming); and we're both fairly driven, achievement-oriented writers. Albom had been Morrie's student in college, and is pretty honest about saying he found the professor and the sociology course he taught way too "touchy-feely" for him; I remember that in my circle of friends, we thought the whole sociology department was one big gut course. But the similarities end there, and not only because I can't think of a single professor who would serve as my Morrie were I to need to find one. I completely lose patience with Mitch Albom because I don't buy that even he buys what he's selling: I don't get the impression that he's any more comfortable with all this touchy-feely stuff than he ever was and, well, I don't like him very much. Say what you will about books like *Traveling Mercies* or the hundreds of how-to-be-at-peace tomes that come across my desk at the office, at least they read like the authors believe what they're saying. *Morrie*, on the other hand, comes off as a cynical attempt to cash in on the spiritual self-improvement movement. I also don't believe that a middle-class, forty-something, Brandeis-educated writer had to travel weekly across the country to learn the kinds of rules that were posted on Charley's kindergarten classroom wall. In all his years as a struggling writer, through his own marriage and inevitable, universal interpersonal problems, had he never been told to slow down, share love, or seize the day? If not, then I feel sorry for Albom and worry at the state of American parenting today.

Speaking of parenting, the whole time I'm reading *Tuesdays*, Charley is snoring softly beside me, one half-fist thrown casually over my shoulder. (Another reason I love Maria: While I was forgoing Penelope Leach to read Philip Roth, she was probably holed up with Anita Brookner, and so neither of us worries when eight-year-olds occasionally sleep in the same bed as their parents.) As I often do late at night, I stroke his beautiful round face and whisper silly endearments in his ear. But looking at him tonight, in a wine-and-*Morrie*-induced haze, I start wondering if I've been teaching him the right life lessons, or enough of them.

I think I spend plenty of time and energy imparting my own style of humanistic wisdom to Charley, and I often hear my parents' warnings against conspicuous consumption, meanness, and greed come out of my own mouth. From the time he was old enough to talk—which meant to whine and complain that he didn't have every single one of the action figures he wanted—I developed my mantra. "You know, Charley . . ." it always begins. "I know, Mom," he learned to say early and often, in pitch-perfect mother imitation, "there are other people in the world and you must learn to appreciate the privileges you've got."

So it's not that I worry that Charley will grow up mean or angry or nasty; he's a pretty good-natured kid, if unbelievably stubborn, and his teachers so far have all commented on his unusually mature sense of empathy. But neither Leo nor I practice any particular religion, and it occurs to me that we might need to work harder to make sure he gets at home the basic messages he'd get at church or temple.

It occurs to me, too, that we'd better start soon, before Charley grows up to be a forty-year-old man content to seek out and be satisfied with the easy lessons in this book.

November 15

Oeuvre and Oeuvre Again

O nce upon a time, an editor friend gave me a book. It was a big book—850 pages—and it was by a writer I'd never heard of, a Dutch-born Brit named Michel Faber. The book, *The Crimson Petal and the White*, was "the best" the editor had ever published, she said, but I didn't pay too much attention to that, because she's the hyperbolic type and has said that to me at least a half-dozen times in the half-dozen years of our acquaintance. Still, after I opened the book in the cab on the way home from my lunch with my friend and read a few pages, I was so enthralled I knew immediately what I had to do. I had to put the book away and not think of it again until I had a week to hibernate with it. As a woman who's been through her fair share of whirlwind book romances, I knew that to get involved with Faber would mean days of no sleep, of stolen moments, of passion and obsession.

But last week I was ready. I'd been on some disappointing

dates—with *Tuesdays with Morrie* and others—and I was ripe to hook up with a book that would take my breath away. I pulled *Crimson Petal* down from the high shelf on which I'd hidden it from myself and began to read.

A week later, I was still reading. I probably would have been finished if I weren't a chronic dieter with a tendency to dole out my treats. The story of Sugar—see? Faber knew that she'd be addictive—the Victorian prostitute with a brain rather than a heart of gold, and William, her patron and lover, was so delicious I could allow myself only a little bit at a time. Two more chapters and then you just have to take a shower, I told myself on Saturday morning. Another five pages and then it's time to go to work, I insisted on Monday. Even Charley, who has taken on some of his father's obliviousness to my weirder reading habits, noticed something was up. "You usually leave books open all over the house," he said, obviously having noticed my double-booking, "but you keep carrying this one everywhere we go."

As you know, I've fallen in love with books and their authors before. So you'll understand how serious my Faber flirtation was when I tell you that I could have no more double-booked on him than . . . well, you follow the metaphor. Even more telling: the first thing I did upon closing *Crimson Petal* was set out to meet the rest of its family. Faber, apparently, also wrote a novel called *Under the Skin*, which came out in 2000; there was no question that I would read that next.

I'm not always an oeuvre reader, or at least not an oeuvre-in-a-row reader. I kind of flit from one topic, one genre, and one author to another, depending on my mood and what's going on around

me and also, to some extent, what's in the nearest pile at three
A.M. Call me fickle, but in the same way that I hesitate to reread,
I'm too impatient to stick with one author for weeks at a time: I
want to get on to the next thing. And besides, sometimes reading
a writer's books back to back can be like scheduling a second, or
third, or fourth date too close to the first: you get such a rush of information and some of it is stuff you don't necessarily want to
know, at least not so soon.

That's what happened between me and Paul Watkins, for example. I first "met" Paul through *Archangel*, his weird novel about
an environmentalist and a logger in the American Northwest; I remember loving it especially because it had some strange characters
and subplots, one involving the local crazy woman whom towns-
people called Mary the Clock. "This is great stuff!" I remember
thinking, as I trudged out to the bookstore to find everything else
my new beloved had ever written. "I need more." But I never got
past the first thirty pages of *The Story of My Disappearance*, and to
judge from the lineup of uncracked Watkins spines on my shelves,
I never opened the others. For me, Watkins made a great first impression, but to get to know him was, I'm afraid, to get over him.

Still, I've certainly "done" a writer's whole body of work before
and enjoyed it. There's Philip Roth, of course, who, as far as I'm
concerned, can never write enough. Through the decades when
many friends told me they'd taken a Roth sabbatical—"too mean,"
some say; "too sex-obsessed," according to others—I've faithfully
read every one of his books; I may have found some titles harder
to get into than others, but I'm endlessly fascinated by his ability
to tell the same story of Jewish dislocation again and again. Ditto,

Diane Johnson's novels (but not the nonfiction); there's something about her obsession with the clash of cultures that resonates with me. And when I discovered Elinor Lipman's *Isabel's Bed*, back in the mid-nineties, I knew I'd found a soul mate in what some critics have called the "contemporary Jane Austen." Not only did I immediately go out and read all her previous novels, including her best and first, *And Then She Found Me*, but I still make sure to read the subsequent ones as soon as they're published. Even though they're not all spectacular, I feel closer to Lipman with every book; because she's like a friend from childhood with whom your relationship ebbs and flows, I can recognize and forgive the inevitable flaws and false steps because I've been walking along with her for so long.

It's a truism—some might say a tragedy—about contemporary publishing that a successful writer needs to become a brand, like Kleenex: you write one book that establishes your sensibility and themes, and then you have to write that book over and over again. That's clearly the secret behind the success of, say, Mary Higgins Clark and John Grisham and Tom Clancy and Robert Ludlum; Ludlum is so well established as a brand that there are still books coming out under his name (written from "notes" and with an "editor") although he died back in 2001. And even many so-called more serious writers seem to write the same book multiple times to continued success. Look at Caleb Carr, who made a name for himself with *The Alienist* and then turned around to write virtually the same bestselling book—a historical thriller with social and political undertones—in *The Angel of Darkness*. (And then look at the failure of his *Killing Time*, a foray into sci-fi horror; you can look at it, but almost nobody else did.) The list is very long: David McCullough (impossibly detailed historical portraits); Kathryn Harrison (turgid tales of forbidden sexuality, whether fiction or no); Anita Shreve (upscale romance); among many others. "It's just easier this way," one editor told me recently. "Readers like to know what they're going to get."

Maybe it was ever thus. There's a school of thought that insists even Dickens and Edith Wharton wrote the same novels of manners time and again. But where does that theory leave, say, Truman Capote? On one recent morning, I curled up in bed with *Breakfast at Tiffany's* while Charley watched SpongeBob SquarePants on Nickelodeon. Having not read the book in years (and having seen the movie ages ago), I was struck by its gentleness, and the fact that the original portrait of Holly Golightly was a lot sadder and darker than Audrey Hepburn ever implied; how could this possibly have come from the same author who wrote *In Cold Blood?* The subject matter and tone couldn't be more different, and yet when I looked at the true-crime masterpiece, I realized the two did have something in common: they both contained exquisitely detailed portraits of people on the edge of society, and both created an almost unbearably recognizable sense of place. They're very different books, but there is a thread that connects them.

Still, I pity poor authors. Either they go ahead and write what they want, and what they know, and what the masses—if the number of people in this country who buy books are enough to qualify as one mass, let alone more than one—want them to write, and then a wiseguy like me comes along and calls them one-trick ponies. Or worse, somebody takes a flier and tries to write something different or strange or unexpected, and that same wiseguy feels betrayed. "What happened to the man I loved?" I would have wailed to Paul Watkins.

Maybe the point is, as Vladimir Nabokov once said, that good writers should imitate only themselves, in different forms, but that doesn't mean they should try out sensibilities like so many jackets at an after-Christmas sale. Maybe it's best, at least for us persnickety readers, when a writer has one set of subjects or themes that he revisits in different ways over time. Or at least that's what I told myself as I opened Faber's *Under the Skin* and began to read about this weird race of creatures, part animal, part human, who abduct and kill full humans, whom they call "vodsels," and sell them off for meat. But for a long while, I was having trouble associating this tense and edgy sci-fi-ish novel—which reminded me of *Animal Farm*, Jonathan Lethem's *Girl in Landscape*, and a weird dogs-asking book called *The Lives of the Monster Dogs*—with the languorous, lush, and Dickensian *Crimson Petal and the White*. "Be careful," the editor of the last had told me when I called to say I was going out to get *Under the Skin*. "It's very different."

I'll say. *Crimson Petal* is about a whore and her lover, and its venue is class-defined nineteenth-century England. It has a few subplots (though true Dickens lovers say it doesn't begin to have enough) about the businessman's brother, his servants, and his long-suffering wife. *Under the Skin*, on the other hand, is a seemingly straightforward narrative about an apparent female who has been surgically altered and forced to be a murderer; it's set in a vague future. One is a historical; the other an allegory. And yet, eventually, I began to see a flicker of connection between the two:

while set in different times and written in different styles, both books explore the cruelties of society, the viciousness of sex, and the subversion of women. Both clearly reflect Faber's sensibility—and he's one sick, you should forgive the expression, puppy.

It's worth pointing out, though, that I read the Faber oeuvre in the exact opposite order in which it was written (or at least published: articles about the forty-two-year-old author say he has been working on the Victorian opus off and on for twenty years), so any conclusions I may draw about his emerging sensibility could be backward, too. If you read Roth in order, for example, you clearly see what reviewers would call the "maturing" of the author from a sex-obsessed Jewish boy (*Portnoy's Complaint; Goodbye, Columbus*) to a sex-obsessed old Jewish man (*The Dying Animal*). Reading Kathryn Harrison in order, from *Thicker Than Water* (a novel about a young woman's consensual affair with her father) through *The Kiss* (a memoir about her own consensual affair with her father) through *The Seal Wife* (about a mute Inuit woman who has an affair but doesn't speak about it or anything else), you can imagine that she's slowly working through her demons. With Faber, the fact that *Crimson Petal* does not end disastrously—he told one interviewer that he killed Sugar off in an earlier draft; here, she simply disappears from William's home—suggests he has come a ways since his bleak, black view of the world portrayed in *Under the Skin.*

But then again, maybe I'm overthinking, and just trying to make excuses for the guy I've decided this week that I love. I do that with all my paramours, I realize: give them the benefit of the doubt even when their behavior is weird and they start scaring me.

Had Leo been in one of his black moods the night I met him, I doubt I would have been interested. But like Faber, he hooked me with his very best self right from the start. In reading as in life, first impressions count: they're what make you stick around for the rest of the story.

November 25

Openings

Speaking of first impressions, publishers believe in them, too. A lot. In fact, you might be amazed to learn just how much they think your purchase patterns have to do with titles and jacket design, and sometimes even blurbs. An enormous amount of time and discussion goes into choosing those titles and covers, which is depressing when you realize that so many of the books you like often have the worst of both. (*Facing the Wind? Slammerkin?*) Sitting here looking at my piles, I try to divorce myself from what I know about the books inside and just concentrate on the jackets. Hmm, could I get away with blaming my ho-hum reaction to *Hammett* on the fact that the cover was so dark and the grainy photo of the writer so vague that the last thing I felt was compelled. But then, look at the fuzzy cover and terrible title on *House of Sand and Fog*, one of my very favorites: it's so dark and dreary I might have mistaken it for a horror novel.

Because a lot of times I have the opportunity to choose books before they even have covers, I'm usually not swayed one way or another by design. And I'm often amazed when I go into a bookstore and see something I read in proof all dressed up and ready to sell: "That's what they put on the cover?" I'll often think. I might have had a completely different image in mind. Clearly, then, I'm not the best person to ask about what jackets should look like, and I've learned over the years not to try to judge a book by its cover.

On the other hand, I'm more than happy to start judging it at its first line.

As I discovered last week, *The Miracle Life of Edgar Mint* has a great one: "If I could tell you only one thing about my life it would be this: when I was seven years old the mailman ran over my head." Who could resist such an opening? It has mystery and violence and pathos. It suggests—no, it advertises—that the story to come will be filled with humor and heart. It does what every writer, and every publisher, wants a first line to do: it draws the reader in.

A sentence like that should be parsed and examined and taught in writing classes all over the country, or at least in writing classes that concern themselves with getting their students published.

The Miracle Life of Edgar Mint is a first novel by a writer named Brady Udall, who found some critical success a couple of years ago with a short-story collection called *Letting Loose the Hounds.* It's about Edgar Mint, an accident-prone half-Apache orphan who somehow manages to survive a life full of comic disasters, the likes of which we haven't seen since John Irving's *The World According to Garp* or Wally Lamb's *She's Come Undone* or maybe even John Kennedy Toole's *A Confederacy of Dunces,* though I have to admit that I'm basing that last part of the statement on some vague recollections of stuff I read about *Dunces*, having never actually read the book itself.

In other words, it's a big, sprawling picaresque that, now that I'm done with it, I'd say delivers on its promised humor and heart. But I wavered there for about a hundred pages in the middle, and for a few not-so-brief-or-shining moments, I considered dumping it altogether like all those other well-reviewed but impenetrable (to me) tomes I've already told you about. Toward the middle of the book, I felt that the raw energy of the opening turned just plain raw. Is it me or is there just a bit too much of what my grandmother would have called bathroom humor? It seems, for pages and pages, that Edgar and his friends can't stop referring to the "shithouse," playing really, really gross and violent pranks on one another (one has to do with inserting a string in a very private place and then setting it on fire), and calling one another "retard." I mean, I'm the mother of an eight-year-old; I know how boys are . . . but geez. I could almost hear Jack Nicholson from *A Few Good Men* booming in my ear, "You want the truth about boys? You can't *handle* the truth."

But unlike virtually every other adult in Edgar's life, I didn't abandon him, believing somehow that the wit and pathos of his original voice would return to save us both. That's the good news about a good first line: Like the romantic insanity of the first weeks of a love affair, it can ground you, and keep you from bolting later on when things calm down. But there's risk in opening big, too: A powerful beginning raises a reader's hopes. Should the rest of the book not measure up—and let's face it, so few do—I feel ripped off.

Hell hath no fury like an expectant reader scorned.

Publishers know this, of course, and the smart ones try to head disappointment off at the pass. As I was starting to drag through the middle of *Edgar Mint*, I turned to look at the copy on the back cover. (My version, which I found at the bottom of a pile that had been sitting in my office for a year, was what publishers call an advance reading copy, which is just like the real book except not proofread, and sometimes with a different cover. ARCs are not all that common for paperbacks—reaching out to reviewers and booksellers and other big-mouths usually comes only at the hard-cover stage—but it so happened that this one came that way.) There, on Vintage Books letterhead, was a note from the novel's paperback editor, Marty Asher. "When I read the opening lines of *The Miracle Life of Edgar Mint*. . . . I knew I was a goner," Asher writes, before reproducing the entire first paragraph. And then he goes on: "All of us at Vintage are Edgar Mint fanatics and *if this letter simply gets you to read past that amazing first paragraph*, then I have no doubt that you will be a goner too." I put those thirteen words in italics (Asher didn't, of course) because when I read them, mid-slog, it suddenly hit me that the editor knew what I knew: the best stuff was at the beginning.

If, as the saying goes, every journey begins with a single step, every book begins with a single sentence—and I think that the more enticing that sentence, the better. Would you have dragged through *Moby-Dick* (if, that is, you ever did drag through it) if it had begun with a convoluted explanation of whaling instead of the simple statement: "Call me Ishmael"? Would generations of re-luctant high school readers ever complete their summer reading requirement, *A Tale of Two Cities,* were it not for the provocative "It was the best of times, it was the worst of times"?

I'm supposed to be a sophisticated reader. I'm supposed to know better. But like the very experienced Marty Asher, I too can get besotted with a great first line. Here are some that belong in my very own First Line Hall of Fame:

The first time I had sex with a man for money, it was September.

—LAURA KASISCHKE, *Suspicious River*

I have noticed that when someone asks for you on the telephone and, finding you out, leaves a message begging you to call him up the moment you come in, as it's important, the matter is more often important to him than to you.

—W. SOMERSET MAUGHAM, *Cakes and Ale*

My name was Salmon, like the fish; first name, Susie. I was fourteen when I was murdered.

—ALICE SEBOLD, *The Lovely Bones*

I am always drawn back to places where I have lived, the houses and their neighborhoods.

—TRUMAN CAPOTE, *Breakfast at Tiffany's*

It was love at first sight.

—JOSEPH HELLER, *Catch-22*

Sara Nelson

It is a truth universally acknowledged that a single man in possession of a good fortune must be in want of a wife.

—JANE AUSTEN, *Pride and Prejudice*

Many years later, as he faced the firing squad, Colonel Aureliano Buendía was to remember that distant afternoon when his father took him to discover ice.

—GABRIEL GARCÍA MÁRQUEZ, *One Hundred Years of Solitude*

See what I mean? *The Miracle Life of Edgar Mint* is in mighty fine company.

December 10
Friends and Family

I can't tell you the title of the book I read last week because, well, it doesn't have a title. In fact, it's not even officially a book yet; it's just a pile of 250 typewritten pages in search of a publisher. The author, Peggy, is a friend of mine, one of my very favorite people in the world, but one who would tell you on first meeting that she is not, professionally or temperamentally, a writer. On Friday, she called and asked me if I'd look at her manuscript. And then she uttered the two most dangerous sentences in the English language. "Tell me the truth," she said. "Please be honest."

Tell me the truth. That's what Charley said earlier this month when we began planning our Christmas visit to Liza's house. "There's no Santa Claus, right, Mom?" he said. "Just tell me the truth."

"Hmm," I said.

The next day, he said it again. "Mom, tell me the truth: you're Santa Claus, right?"

I tried some lame humor: "You callin' me a fat guy in a red suit?" I said.

He didn't laugh.

"Tell me the truth, Mom. Don't you buy all the presents?"

I bobbed and wove. "You think I buy *all* those presents?" I asked. "I'm not made of money, you know."

Having heard that remark a few hundred times before, he seemed satisfied. Santa Claus case: closed, at least for now.

Would that my writer friends were eight-year-olds who didn't know about nondenial denials.

If a book recommended between friends is not so much a book as a pop quiz, a request to read someone's unpublished manuscript is like the law boards, the med boards, and the FBI clearance exams all rolled into one. You're being called on for your expertise in a given area, but if you don't give the tester the answer she wants, you risk expulsion. The only good news is that you usually have time to prepare your answers. How honest should you be? A novelist friend who's had her fair share of similar requests has worked up a theorem: Grade your degree of closeness to the person on a scale of 1 to 10, then divide that number by how good or bad you think the book is (also 1 to 10). "And then tell them you love it," she says.

As a writer, I subscribe to the bartender theory of manuscript sharing: Like the unhappy husband who confides his misery to the guy pouring the beer or the stranger sitting next to him on the train, I'm much more comfortable spilling my guts—what Anne Lamott calls my "shitty first [and second and third] drafts"—to people outside my immediate circle. If a second- or third-tier friend likes what I've written, I can tell myself her reaction was "pure" because her personal involvement with me is minimal, and if she hates it, I can dismiss what she says because I don't have to face her in the morning. If this is what Peggy is doing, I know what my job is: to follow my friend's theorem and tell her it's great. But what if, like Charley, she really wants to know "the truth," and "the truth" is that I think the book's a mess?

These were the questions that occupied me from three to five A.M. Saturday morning and a good chunk of the next afternoon as I combed through Peggy's memoir. And for a while, I was plenty worried. Peggy is not, as I said, an experienced writer—and for the first fifty pages I agonized over whether I should tell even this tough, forthright woman that she should probably bag the whole project. But then, on about page 60, the book began to change; it actually started to become a book, because Peggy started to speak passionately in her own voice about the people she'd known and the lessons she'd learned. "I think what you need to do is throw out the first fifty pages and forget about the last fifty pages," I told her when I called her on Monday. "And then work on what you've got in the middle."

"So you don't think it's a total disaster?" she said.

"No," I said. Whew, I thought.

Worried as I was about reading Peggy's manuscript, I realized later that this situation was nothing compared with the one Liza and I got ourselves into a couple of years back. Liza had been "working on" a novel for, oh, I don't know, maybe for as long as I'd known her, and for several of the more recent years I'd been asking her to let me see it. She kept demurring, and then one day, more or less out of the blue, she offered to send it to me. "Great!" I said. "Please tell me the truth," she said.

I should have been nervous. Hell, I should have been petrified. This was my sister, of whose intellect I've always been afraid and jealous. What if I hated it and told her "the truth" and our relationship, which had survived some bad years there back in adolescence but was definitely on an upswing in recent decades, collapsed around me? Or what if I loved it and was so consumed by all the envy and jealousy I go around trying to pretend I don't have that I couldn't talk to her? There was no way, I should have realized, that this wouldn't end badly. Liza and I come from a clan that has historically mixed business with family—to disastrous results: both my grandfather and my father started companies with their brothers, and both died estranged from those brothers. Getting involved with Liza and her novel had a good chance of becoming another version of *Bleak House*.

Except it didn't. In fact, it turned out to be more like a remake of *Rich and Famous*. Here was an opportunity for both of us to play to our strengths and stick to our prescribed roles. Liza, the artist, had written the book, and I, the more commercially minded critic, could help her get it into shape, get it to an editor, and get it published. She was happy to have the help and I was thrilled to be useful: it was a match that could have been made in film heaven.

Of course, it helped that when I read the novel—*Playing Botticelli*, it's called; it was published in 2000—I just plain loved it. Well, okay, I had a couple of problems with it—like, I remember, some feeling that the love interest in the book wasn't completely believable and that he needed to be redrawn—but they were the kinds of minor problems that (a) she could easily fix if she wanted to or (b) I wouldn't feel dissed if she didn't. And she, for her part, was a willing listener: I remember her pronouncing me "a genius" when I suggested that if she made the hero a farrier (a guy who shoes horses, if you didn't know; like Godiva Blue, *Botticelli*'s heroine, Liza lives a rural life), the love affair would make more sense. When she'd made the changes, I started talking it up to editors and agents I knew, as did others of her friends, and eventually it landed with a woman I'd worked with for many years. The book was published, and we both ended up with what we wanted: she was a bona fide novelist, and I had been the successful helpmeet. Any jealousy I might have felt was mitigated by a sense of a tiny bit of ownership.

Looking back on the *Playing Botticelli* period now, I think it should be taught as a test case in writerly sisterhood. Liza had waited until she was truly ready to let someone else read it, and when she said "Tell me the truth," she actually meant it. Ever the little sister, I entered into the whole thing with the desire to please her, but also to show that I was actually an independent smart person whose years on the reader end of the publishing business might be of use to her. At her book party, let's just say, we were both beaming.

Things don't always work out so well, of course, partly because we're not all tuned in to our real feelings and partly because, even with unpublished books, timing is important. A friend of mine last winter asked me to read his manuscript, which was scheduled to come out in the spring. "Please be honest," he said, "tell me what you really think."

I took the manuscript home for the weekend. I dutifully read it through and (thankfully) laughed where I was supposed to and didn't where I wasn't. I liked the book a lot, although I did think it took too long to get started and that he should probably prune the opening two chapters. Knowing my friend to be the thin-skinned, anxious type—did I mention he is a professional writer?—I agonized about what to do. Should I tell him I thought the opening was slow?

"Tell me what you really think," he had said. So on Monday morning, I did. "It's great, it's hilarious, I love it," I told him. "But if I were you, I'd cut back on the opening a little."

Silence on the other end of the line. "I can't really do that," he said. "It's in copyedit."

In a masterstroke of timing, my friend had given me his manuscript to read when it was already bought, accepted, and in the later stages of the publishing process.

I was annoyed, to say the least. "You set me up!" I said. "How dare you give me something that's completely finished and then demand that I tell you what I really think!"

"I shouldn't have done that," he conceded.

I thought, of course, that he meant he shouldn't have given me the manuscript so late. I felt vindicated. And then it was his time to tell me "the truth"—a truth that most writers don't have the nerve to say out loud, even to the most well-meaning and wisely critical friends.

"I just wanted you to say it was brilliant," he said. "I didn't want you to tell me what you *really* think."

December 30
What Did I Do?[7]

You'd think that by now I'd know better. You'd think that after a year of compiling lists and packing for trips and trying to control my reading life, I'd have figured out that it is uncontrollable. Still, as John Belushi used to say (and as Leo and I often say to each other, in one of the few *Saturday Night Live* catchphrases we ever use), "But noooooooo." I'm just back from a few days with the family at Liza's, and once again I'd gotten the book thing all wrong.

Every year for the past two decades, I've gone—either alone or with friends and now with Charley and Leo—to Liza's Georgia farm to celebrate Christmas the way only two Jewish girls can, which is to say extravagantly. As kids, we'd never observed the hol-

---

[7]I stole this title from the late painter and musician Larry Rivers, who used it for his autobiography, a book so frank and hilarious that it's now impossible for me to like any other celebrity memoir.

iday, but as wives of Christians and mothers of kids who celebrate every festival, Jewish or not, that involves food and/or gifts, we go wild. For several days, we bake our brains out, decorate the house and tree with Santa Clauses and red balls and ornaments we've collected over the years, and generally "make merry." We plan and execute an elaborate Christmas Eve dinner, to which Liza invites some of her local friends, after which we all sit up late drinking and playing games of our own idiosyncratic development. (It's no accident that Liza's novel is called *Playing Botticelli*, referring to a word game we played as kids.) Then, when we're all too groggy to talk, we load up a brown paper bag with gifts from Santa and fill the stockings and make sure we leave a plate of cookies and a half-drunk glass of milk for the children to find in the morning. Usually, my mother comes up from Key West for the festivities; sometimes one of my brothers comes, too, and on occasion one of Liza's old friends from school. We're pretty busy, but there always seems to be time to lie around by the fire that Liza's husband, Rick, keeps burning all day, which means, of course, a lot of reading.

So here was my plan: I was going to end the year the way I'd tried to start it—by reading and enjoying Ted Heller's *Funnymen*. It seemed the perfect choice to meet the major requirements. I'd be spending the next days in a jokey, talkative, histrionic group of people—did I mention my mother was going to be there?—some of whom actually remember the Jerry Lewis–Dean Martin days and would surely get the jokes. Even better, finishing the book that I had started at the beginning of the year appealed to my well-documented love of narrative: reading *Funnymen* now would complete the arc.

Except, guess what? I couldn't do it. "What's the matter with you?" Leo asked me the first night, after I'd picked the book up and put it down at least half a dozen times. "Can't you just start where you left off?" But of course, I couldn't: after a year of other authors' pages and plots, I had only a vague memory of *Funnymen*'s first hundred pages, so starting in on page 101 would be like walking into a movie halfway through. On the other hand, the thought of starting from the beginning again was just too daunting. Read something over again, just to get back to where you started? That seemed a ridiculous waste of time. Besides, it almost felt like *Funnymen* was cursed; like a new restaurant on the site of an old restaurant that never had any patrons, it had too much unhappy history. I didn't feel comfortable going there.

You may have noticed by now that in all this year of reading, I've never told you about tackling a book of short stories. That's because—as much as I love pieces by, say, Andre Dubus or Alice Munro when I encounter them singly—I almost never succeed in finishing a whole collection. "Why is that?" I recently asked a friend, who, like many others, has said that short stories are her favorite form of fiction. She told me I had a commitment problem. "When you're beginning a book like a novel, you're entering a writer's world," she told me. "And that takes commitment. With short pieces, you have to make that commitment five or ten separate times in a quick row." Well, *Funnymen* is a problem for me on both counts: it's a novel I have to recommit to, for one thing, and for another, it is written in an oral-history style that is short-story-ish, lots of little pieces, so I have to recommit many times. And that was too intimidating just then.

Still, I really wanted to read this book, and so I set out, the next morning, to find a way into it once and for all. Have you ever been in this desperate state? It seems absurd, really. What's the big deal, I wanted to say, just put the book down, just as you put down *Cold Mountain* and *White Teeth* and that impenetrable Milan Kundera. But wait! my better self responds. You loved *Slab Rat* and you have liked what you've read: before you give up entirely, try the skip-around method of reading, the one where you read the end first and then work your way back to the middle, if not the beginning.

For the first thirty or so years of my life, I would have called this cheating. It was against the rules, and I was nothing if not a follower of rules. To wit: I'm in the fourth grade, and the teacher hands us each a sheet of paper with a dozen questions sandwiched between spaces for the answers. At the top of the page, there's a space to write your name, and then a box marked "Instructions." "Before you write anything, read through the whole test," it says.

Dutifully I get out my number 2 pencil and begin curling the bottom of my braid over my left index finger. I read through the questions and maybe, I confess, doodle some notes to myself about how I will answer them later. (Who was President at the time of the Louisiana Purchase? Jefferson?) I read down through the page, turn it over, and read to the end, where it says: "Good work! Thanks for following the instructions. Do not write anything on this paper except your name at the top and then give it to your teacher." I look around at the other kids, most of whom are filling in the white spaces on their sheets with their newly learned and very labored cursive handwriting. Uh-oh, I think smugly. *Some-*

body isn't following the rules. I, on the other hand, go back and erase my doodles, sign my name, and present the otherwise unmarked paper proudly to the teacher.

I bring this story up not because I think it makes me look so great—in fact, it makes me out to be the kind of Goody Two-shoes teacher-pleaser I was, but am not proud of—or even because, in retrospect, there's something sadistic about the whole incident in the first place. I think I retain such a strong memory of this test because it was one of my first, and very profound, lessons about reading: You have to start at the beginning and get to the end before you're allowed to comment on what came in between. There's an order to these things that you must respect. Beginnings, middles, ends are meant to be beginnings, middles, and ends: confuse them at your own peril.

Little did I know then, or until very recently, that people skip around in books all the time. If I'd thought about it, I would have said only professionals—agents or editors who have major time issues attached to their reading—can be forgiven for doing it. But a couple of years ago I discovered that even my serious sister jumps ahead in a book she reads for pleasure. I found this out by accident, after Liza had been visiting me in New York and had borrowed my copy of Allegra Goodman's great novel *Kaaterskill Falls* to read on the trip home. When she called to check in later that night, she mentioned she'd left the book on the plane. "But it's okay," she said, obviously glossing over the fact that I might have wanted the book back, "I was almost finished, and besides, I'd already read the end." Since then, I've been asking other friends if they ever read out of order, and most, some sheepishly, have said that they do. Why? "Because sometimes I get so anxious from following the plot that I can't concentrate on the language," says one. "Once I know what's going to happen, I can read more patiently."

Frankly, this sounds weird to me, but not quite as weird as the friend who told me he reads backward only in mysteries because he "hates suspense." In my desperation, I tried it with *Funnymen*. Still no luck: *Funnymen* in reverse order was as hard to get into in front of a Georgia fire as in front of a Vermont one. There was just something about the rambunctious, back-and-forth voices of performers, agents, and other vaudevillians that just didn't compel me to keep reading, forth or back. Ted Heller is still, in my book, a good novelist, and I'll be first in line at the store when his next book comes out, but for now, at least, we're parting ways.

The irony isn't lost on me that this is the second time this year that I had to resolve to give up on *Funnymen*. Even more striking: it feels like the second hundredth time I've come face to face with the fact that my best-laid plans rarely end up completed. If I knew it at the beginning of the year, I've learned it ten times over: reading is organic and fluid and pretty unpredictable, based as much on mood and location and timing as anything else. If a book is "good," that doesn't mean you'll want to read it, and if it's "bad," that doesn't mean you'll pass it by. I only have to glance at my original list to see that, in spades. Why didn't I read *Infinite Jest* as I said I would? Because Charley played baseball and because Leo and I had a fight. Because I was feeling nostalgic for my father and visiting with my mother. Because one of my new friends lent me a novel. I couldn't have predicted that those things would happen, let alone when, so I couldn't plan my reading list around them.

But my subconscious mind—the part I've heard writers call the lizard brain—could and did: it told me to reach for Anne Lamott or Edith Wharton or Calvin Trillin instead. And if I've learned one thing in my decades on earth, it's this: Don't argue with your lizard brain; it knows you better than you know yourself.

There was some freedom in this realization, I must admit; it wasn't unlike the way I felt all those months ago when I just gave up on *Ulysses* and *Invisible Man* et al. and went out to buy clothes. And as I did then, I had the feeling that if I could just relax into the fact that I wasn't reading, something would present itself to me as clearly as *Bird by Bird* did last spring. But what? I prowled Liza's shelves—but to no avail, even though there were plenty of titles in English in this particular rural home. While I still think one needs a book to protect oneself from intense intrusions of the familial or any other kind, maybe, just maybe, I would get through this family holiday without a book to protect or distract me. Besides, I still had a lot of cooking to do.

So that's how I came to spend my last official week of my book-reading year with nothing to read. Instead, I endured the usual jokes from my nephew about the time I forgot to put the flour in the peanut butter cookie dough, and went head to head with my mother, who, while Liza and I were out at the store, took it upon herself to reorganize the household refrigerator. And I have to admit, it wasn't so bad. For once I even could see the wisdom in Leo's response to all those Japanese-American books I tried to get him to read: maybe for just a little while I didn't need to read books that would explicate my life. I could just live it.

Besides, there were plenty of stories and characters right in front of me at the Christmas Eve dinner table. There was Mom, who by example and recommendation had made me into the person I am. There was Liza, my lifelong partner in crime, without whom I might never have read Jane Austen and hundreds and hundreds of other books. And, of course, there were Leo and Charley, both of whom have been my affectionate reading foils for years, and who, for all their own needs and interests and schedules, only occasionally told me to knock it off when I nattered on about stuff they knew nothing about and about which they cared less. These are the people I read for, because of, and about, and they're all here in front of me. Suddenly I shocked myself with a wayward, maverick thought: the question "So who needs books at a time like this?" actually crossed my mind.

But don't worry, it didn't stay long. By the time Leo and Charley and I had arrived back in New York, I was myself again. Did I mention that it's three A.M., and I'm wandering my library in my pajamas, looking for something to read? Well, I am, and as always I've got some ideas. Maybe, I think, I should reread *American Pastoral*, the prizewinning novel by Philip Roth that I remember summing up, brilliantly, the experience of a Jewish-American family not unlike my own. But then, as will always happen if you wait long enough, the imaginary spotlight landed on an old book I read years ago. The book was Anne Tyler's *The Accidental Tourist*, which, to many, may conjure up images of the William Hurt–Geena Davis movie. To me it will always be a book about a bunch of kooky relatives adjusting to midlife; remembering the last few days in the kitchen in Georgia, I suddenly feel particularly close to one of Tyler's characters, the sister who feels the need to alphabetize her canned goods.

I read just enough to get sleepy, and then I get up and go back to the bedroom, where Charley has wedged himself into the middle of our double bed and is now snoring lightly beside Leo.

Tomorrow I'll go to the bookstore, I think.

Maybe I've finally rubbed off on Leo a little bit; before he went to bed, he asked me to get him a book.

He wants a copy of *Dr. Atkins' New Diet Revolution*, he said.

It's nothing I would have picked for him. But hey, it's a start.

Epilogue

few days after my reading year ended, I went to dinner with a friend I hadn't seen since around the time it started. We were having a leisurely drink at a bar, talking over the events of the previous year, which in my case amounted to a lot of name dropping of book titles. Eventually, she asked me what I was planning to do next weekend.

"I think I'll take Charley to the museum," I told her.

"Natural History?" she asked.

"No, MoMA, the Museum of Modern Art," I said. "He likes looking at the Pollocks."

"Well, that'll be fun: a quick day trip over to Queens," she said.

"Queens? MoMA is on Fifty-third Street," I said. Right around the corner from where we were sitting, in fact.

"Sara," she said, looking mildly alarmed, "it has been closed for renovations for the past six months. All the exhibits are in temporary quarters in Queens. The debate over this has been all over the TV news and in the papers. A campaign for the new site has been plastered in the subway stations and on the buses. Where have you been?"

Where had I been? I preferred to think of the question as Where hadn't I been? Since beginning My Year of Reading Dangerously, I've been to Vermont, Key West, Fire Island, and Atlanta, if you want names of places to which I'd taken trains and planes. But I've also been to nineteenth-century London and 1980s Wall Street and twenty-first-century heaven. I've met powerhouse newspaper editors, self-destructive drug addicts, charming and unscrupulous financiers, and a couple of adulterous wives. I've also spent a lot of time with the real and remembered people in my life: with Charley, and Leo, and my mother and sister and brothers and late father, and with many dear friends.

But there's a lot I haven't done, a lot of places I haven't gone. I didn't take a major vacation last year, and I saw only a very few movies. I went to the theater only once, when my niece Rosie was in town, and I obviously haven't set foot in a gallery. To tell the truth, I've been lost in more than a couple of conversations with people who tend to make references to new restaurants, important magazine articles, and popular TV shows; can you believe I've never seen *Friends*?

Not that I'm complaining. I've lived the past year exactly how I've wanted to—between the covers of books and in the places in my head that those books have taken me. I've been agitated, excited, enthralled, annoyed, frustrated, and sometimes a little bored.

But I've never been lonely. As my friend Bonnie pointed out on New Year's Day, to read a book is to have a relationship. And I've had dozens of them in the past dozen months.

But maybe it's not such a bad thing that I'm now "done" with my project. Maybe it's time to get back to real life. *They moved the museum.* What else happened when I was too buried in my books to notice? I know that Charley grew a couple of inches and mastered multiplication and that Leo finished a couple of extracurricular projects. I understand that George Bush is still president and that we're on the verge of war. I'm aware that the magazine that employs me continues to publish and, miraculously in this terrible economy, has even grown. But I know, too, that a lot of other important things happened in the world and in my family's life while I sat in my library in the middle of the night and read about other worlds and other lives.

That's, of course, both the good news and the bad news about reading: it takes you away from, as a great writer once said, your "proscribed little here to a vast and intriguing there."[8] And while I certainly did discover, this past year, that there were all sorts of connections between my world and the ones that authors have been creating for centuries, there's also a lot to be learned by taking a break, by closing the book and looking around at actual, not invented, people and places.

How was your year? People have been asking me lately. Did you enjoy yourself? Would you do it again? At first, I was as mystified by these questions as I was when they asked me how in the

---

[8]Just kidding about the "great writer" bit. See "Great Expectations."

world I would ever do it in the first place. "Of course I'd do it again," I say, if "it" means walking into a bookstore or a library or a friend's house or an editor's office and letting myself be called to by the piles of paper printed with ink. Obviously, I can no more stop reading that I can stop eating, even if the latter would be more beneficial to my thighs.

But maybe it's time to slow it down a little, to stop, as Mitch Albom might say, and smell the roses and talk to the husband and watch some TV shows. Maybe it's time to take myself off a schedule for a change. Maybe it's time to take a reading break.

I set out to read "whatever I wanted" and ended up with a reading list I could never have devised. I couldn't have predicted, say, that *A Million Little Pieces* would turn up at the exact moment I needed it, or that spending some time with my mother would reintroduce me to *Marjorie Morningstar*. I had all the best intentions: to read a lot of nonfiction, to pay attention to poetry, to fill in at least some of the holes in my education. But as you can see from these pages, and from Appendix B, I never got to *John Adams*, or to Keats; I couldn't even finish *Funnymen*. For a contrarian and a control freak, realizing that even my preferred pastime was out of my conscious control was a mighty revelation.

How was your year? people want to know.

"It was *great!*" I tell them. And it was. It was also complicated. I was all over the emotional map, and for every moment that was exhilarating, there was one that was frustrating. For every reading experience that was edifying, there was one that was elusive. And just as I thought I had a handle on what I was doing and how important it all was, I realized I was as clueless as ever.

They moved the museum.

A truly great writer would have known how to answer all those probing questions about the past year.

"It was the best of times," he would have said. "It was the worst of times."

Ever the planner, I sat down a couple of days before beginning my reading year and made up this list of how at least to start. I knew there'd be other books, but I meant to begin with some clear intentions.

The Autobiography of Malcolm X. I was too young when it came out, in 1964, and skipped over it in college when tastes ran more to, say, *Zen and the Art of Motorcycle Maintenance.*

Cakes and Ale. My mother was a big Somerset Maugham freak, and I'd read *Razor's Edge* and *Of Human Bondage,* so this one left a hole.

The House of Mirth. The homework I didn't do in college.

A Tale of Two Cities. Ditto.

One Hundred Years of Solitude. The most important book for a Latin American Studies major to have read in the 1980s. I did my duty, but since I read it in Spanish, I didn't retain all that much.

Madame Bovary. As an AP French student in high school, I'd had to read Balzac's *Père Goriot*, but somehow was never assigned this classic. It's probably just as well, since a woman I know who did read it in college French says that her command of the language was so sketchy that she never knew Emma commits suicide.

In Cold Blood. Never read it, never—if you can believe it—saw the movie.

Empire Falls. I'd started the Richard Russo novel when a publisher sent me an advance reader's copy, but got waylaid with something else around page 75. By the time I got back to it, I'd forgotten what had happened so far, and besides, it had just won the Pulitzer and all that attendant hype.

Gravity's Rainbow, because all so-called smart people are supposed to read Pynchon.

The complete, or almost complete, oeuvre of Philip Roth. He's one of my favorites, and I haven't missed any. I even liked *Sabbath's Theater.* So sue me.

John Adams. Am I the only person in America who hasn't read the McCullough classic? I told myself I was waiting for the paperback, which has now arrived.

Some biography of Dorothy Parker, who obsessed me, as she did most would-be writers who grew up on *The New Yorker.*

Restoration, by Rose Tremain, because I loved her *Sacred Country.*

Infinite Jest, by David Foster Wallace. See *Gravity's Rainbow.* Insert the word "hip" before "smart."

Any early novel by Stephen King. Lots of people say he's the most underrated writer around. Marty Asher, publisher of Vintage Books, told me King is this generation's Maugham—too prolific and too readable to be taken seriously in his lifetime.

The Spy Who Came In from the Cold. A confession: I've never read John le Carré. Clearly, I need a reality check.

Snowblind, by Robert Sabbag, because it's a classic piece of journalism about a cocaine smuggler and because Bob is one of my dearest friends. This is one of the few books I regularly reread.

Call It Sleep, by Henry Roth, a novel about Jewish immigrants at the turn of the twentieth century that was rereleased a few years ago. A foray into my roots.

Beloved, by Toni Morrison, which it shames me to admit I haven't read.

Leaves of Grass, by Walt Whitman, because I remain chronically, deeply poetry-challenged.

The Collected Stories of Alice Munro, because my mother talks about them all the time, except that sometimes she gets them confused with the works of Alice McDermott.

From Beirut to Jerusalem, by Thomas L. Friedman, because my understanding of the Middle East is woefully inadequate.

Praying for Sheetrock, by Melissa Faye Greene, because six separate people have told me it's an extremely important book.

The Confessions of Nat Turner, by William Styron, because everybody, including me, has read *Sophie's Choice.*

The Chief: The Life of William Randolph Hearst, by David Nasaw, because a review called it "a grand American story." And I'm a sucker for same.

Trainspotting, by Irvine Welsh, because I once lent it, unread, to an acquaintance and insisted on getting it back *within the week* so I could read it. And I never did.

What I Actually Did Read, as of 12/30/02

*S*o did you make your book-a-week goal? people have been
asking me. The real answer: Yes and no. Sometimes I read a
book in a day. Some things took a couple of weeks. And
some that I read I didn't write about. The final tally: a lot more
than fifty-two books, even if I can't name absolutely everything I
dipped into or skimmed through. Here, though, is a partial list of
what I read that I haven't mentioned elsewhere in these pages:

The Danish Girl, by David Ebershoff, a historical novel about a sex
change, which paved the way for a truly amazing sex-change
memoir that is just coming out, called *She's Not There,* by Jennifer
(formerly James) Finney Boylan.

The Anatomy Lesson, one of the few of Philip Roth's books I didn't
remember. I loved it, as usual.

Nickel and Dimed: On (Not) Getting By in America, by Barbara Ehrenreich, because the author is Key West–based, not to mention brilliant.

Loaded, by Robert Sabbag, the latest from my friend. Given the time constraints I chose to read this instead of *Snowblind*—again.

Random Family, by Adrian Nicole Leblanc, which in my opinion will become the *There Are No Children Here* of its time.

The Only Girl in the Car, by Kathie Dobie, a memoir about a promiscuous youth, spent in New Haven, Connecticut, a scene of many of my own crimes.

Cakes and Ale, by Somerset Maugham, which was as good as my mother always told me it was.

Dorothy Parker, by Marion Meade. It was as if I'd waited my whole life for this one.

Think of England, by Alice Elliot Dark, a disappointment after her amazing stories, *In the Gloaming*.

A Boy's Own Story, by Edmund White, a reread, after my letter to Robert Plunket.

Stranger Things Happen, by Kelly Link, a collection of stories so bizarre and inventive I actually broke with tradition and read the whole thing.

Mary Higgins Clark's *You Belong to Me*. What can I say? I had a long plane ride for business and thought I'd experiment with something from the mass market paperback rack. It wasn't bad, although I didn't remember much of it once I'd landed.

The Sisters Mallone, a novel by Louisa Ermelino. She's a friend, but I would have read it and loved it anyway.

I Want That: How We All Became Shoppers, by Thomas Hine, a sociological examination of why we buy things. "Shopping has a lot in common with sex," Hine writes. How could I resist that?

The Ice Storm, by Rick Moody, who gets a bad rap in the New York literary community these days. So maybe it's not PC to say so, but I loved the novel.

Gentlemen's Agreement, by Laura Z. Hobson. You know the Gregory Peck movie? I didn't. But this is one of those books about anti-Semitism every postwar Jew is supposed to have read. It's a little stylized and dated now, but still somehow appropriate.

The Spooky Art, by Norman Mailer. Not so brilliant as, say, *The Executioner's Song*, but it's essays, and he's eighty, which qualifies him, ironically, as a dancing bear again. This time, he's just an old one.

Disgrace, by J. M. Coetzee, a surprisingly readable novel about racism and family in South Africa, proof positive that prize-winners—this won the Booker—are not automatically homework.

Honor Lost, by Norma Khouri, the kind of true-crime even I can't skip: a horrific tale of a contemporary Jordanian Muslim killed by her family because she loved a Christian man.

Joe Gould's Secret, by Joseph Mitchell. Two essays reprinted from *The New Yorker* (twenty years apart) about a homeless man who might or might not have been a literary genius. Its special appeal to Liza and me is that it mentions one of my mother's relatives, Eddie Gottlieb, a newspaperman who was a contemporary of Mitchell's and of Joe Gould's.

American Sphinx. Okay, this was a skim-only, but given that it's by Joseph J. Ellis, who was discredited for lying about his Vietnam service, I wanted to be sure to tell the truth.

Appendix C
The Must-Read Pile, *as of 1/1/03*

S ome things never change—and some books never seem to leave the must-read pile. Here's a snapshot of what's waiting for me beside the bed, now that I can read with no deadlines.

Seabiscuit, by Laura Hillenbrand. What's the matter with me? By now, hundreds of thousands have read the paperback, and my hardcover has barely been cracked.

The Cider House Rules. My friend Adrian was shocked that the only John Irving I can remember reading is *The World According to Garp*.

The Way We Live Now, by Anthony Trollope. I guess I feel heartened by my successful adventures with all those "old books."

East of Eden, by John Steinbeck. I picked it up on the summer reading table at Barnes & Noble last summer. It's been here ever since.

Appendix C

The Pursuit of Alice Thrift, by Elinor Lipman. To judge from my earlier Lipmania, this is one novel I'd bet I'll get to.

From Beirut to Jerusalem, by Thomas L. Friedman. Because my ignorance just isn't forgivable anymore, especially not now.